JAZZ
in
MIND

Jazz History, Culture, and Criticism Series

William H. Kenney III, *Editor*

Books in this series

Jazz in Mind: Essays on the History and Meanings of Jazz, edited by Reginald T. Buckner and Steven Weiland, 1991

JAZZ
in
MIND

ESSAYS on the HISTORY
and MEANINGS of JAZZ

Edited by
Reginald T. Buckner
and
Steven Weiland

Wayne State University Press   Detroit

96 95 94 93 92   5   4   3   2   1

Library of Congress Cataloging-in-Publication Data

Jazz in mind : essays on the history and meanings of jazz / ed-
ited by
Reginald T. Buckner and Steven Weiland.
     p.   cm. — (Jazz history, culture, and criticism series)
   "Most essays in Jazz in mind were initially presented at a
scholarly conference at the University of Minnesota in fall 1987"—
Introd.
   Includes bibliographical references and index.
   ISBN 0-8143-2168-2 (alk. paper)
   1. Jazz–History and criticism.   I. Buckner, Reginald T.
II. Weiland, Steven.   III. Series.
ML3507.J38 1992
781.65'09'04–dc20   91-10851

Book design by Mary Krzewinski

To
our
children

CONTENTS

Contributors   9

Introduction   13
Reginald T. Buckner and Steven Weiland

James Reese Europe and the Prehistory of Jazz   19
R. Reid Badger

Negotiating the Color Line:
Louis Armstrong's Autobiographies   38
William H. Kenney III

Soviet Jazz:
Transforming American Music   60
Greg Gaut

The Problem of Local Jazz History:
The Example of South Carolina   83
Benjamin Franklin V

7

Contents

The Quoter and His Culture 92
Krin Gabbard

"Jazz Isn't Just Me":
Jazz Autobiographies as Performance
Personas 112
Kathy Ogren

Jazz and Modernism:
Changing Conceptions of Innovation and
Tradition 128
Mark S. Harvey

Jazz as Social Structure, Process and Outcome 148
David T. Bastien and Todd J. Hostager

Appendix A:
James Reese Europe, Discography 166

Appendix B:
Soviet Jazz, Discography 174

Appendix C:
Jazz and Modernism, Discography 177

Index 181

CONTRIBUTORS

R. Reid Badger teaches American studies at the University of Alabama. His research interests include early jazz and twentieth-century American culture. His biography of James R. Europe will be published by Oxford University Press.

David T. Bastien holds a Ph.D. from the University of Minnesota. He is assistant professor of communication at the University of Wisconsin–Milwaukee. His essay (with Todd Hostager) is part of a larger project using jazz as a site for social science research. His other research interests include the study of corporate mergers and acquisitions.

Reginald T. Buckner was until his death in 1989 professor of music, jazz studies, and African-American Studies at the University of Minnesota. He was active regionally and nationally in jazz education. He was also a widely published writer on jazz history and a highly regarded pianist and group leader.

Benjamin Franklin V is professor of English at the University of South Carolina. During his twenty years as a jazz writer he has contributed most frequently to *Coda* and *Jazz Forum*. His "Jazz in Retrospect," begun in 1975, is heard throughout much of the Southeast on the South Carolina Educational Radio Network.

Krin Gabbard is associate professor of comparative literature at the State University of New York at Stony Brook. He is senior author of *Psychiatry and the Cinema* (University of Chicago Press, 1987). His articles on literature, film, and other subjects have appeared in many journals. He is currently at work on a book, tentatively titled *Low and High: Jazz and American Culture, 1940–1956*.

Greg Gaut is completing his doctoral dissertation at the University of Minnesota in Russian and Soviet history. His special fields of interest are intellectual history and contemporary Soviet popular culture. He has taught at the University of Minnesota, Gustavus Adolphus College, and Metropolitan State University.

Mark S. Harvey is a composer who teaches jazz studies at the Massachusetts Institute of Technology. He leads the Aardvark Jazz Orchestra, which he founded in 1973. He has performed and recorded with George Russell, Gil Evans, Sheila Jordan, and others. He is the author of essays on music, religion, and culture and is at work on a biography of jazz trumpeter Howard McGhee.

Todd J. Hostager is assistant professor of business administration at the University of Wisconsin–Eau Claire. He is a doctoral candidate in the Program in Strategic Management at the University of Minnesota. His research focuses on the effects of metaphorical thinking on problem formation and problem solving.

William H. Kenney III is associate professor of history and coordinator of the American Studies Program at Kent State University. He is co-editor with Scott Deveaux of *The Music of James Scott* (Smithsonian Institution Press, 1992) and author of *A Racial and Cultural History, 1904–1930*, forthcoming from Oxford University Press.

Kathy Ogren is associate professor of history at the University of Redlands. Her book *The Jazz Revolution: Twenties America and the Meaning of Jazz* (1989) won an ASCAP Deems Taylor Award. She is at work on a book about jazz autobiographies.

Steven Weiland is Professor of Education at Michigan State University. He is the author of *Intellectual Craftsmen: Ways and Works in American Scholarship, 1935–1990* (Transaction Books, 1991) and many essays and reviews in the humanities, social sciences, and education.

INTRODUCTION

Reginald T. Buckner and Steven Weiland

Jazz, our most spontaneous art, does not resist written interpretation, but it has its own ways of welcoming it. Jazz musicians themselves have always insisted on the utterly idiomatic content of the music. In his autobiography jazz critic Nat Hentoff recalls being told at age nineteen by the renowned drummer Jo Jones: "It is time for you to find out what you have to know if you are going to write about this music." Jones's advice is simple: "When you hear a jazz musician on that stand, he is telling you what happened to him this afternoon, the night before, what has happened to him during his whole life. This is serious business. And there is no way a jazz musician, if he is a real jazz musician, can hide any of that, because we play ourselves, not Beethoven or whoever."[1]

With such an appealing if demanding personal standard to aim for it is easy to see why Hentoff moved enthusiastically from a budding but relatively orthodox career in political journalism to the world of music. And Hentoff's own contributions admirably represent Jones's direction; in his pioneering *Hear Me Talkin' To Ya* (in which more jazz voices are added to Jones's) and in other writing he seeks to convey the value of jazz from within the experience of its performers.

It is worth remembering, however, that during the period of Hentoff's critical apprenticeship jazz also entered American intellectual and artistic life on less promising terms. William Carlos Williams, for example, has few rivals in American letters for his grasp of themes of national and local culture. He embarked on both his medical and literary careers during the Jazz Age but later contact with the origins of this country's most indigenous art form did not prevent him from misunderstanding its sources and meanings. When Bunk Johnson, the self-proclaimed tutor of Louis Armstrong, was rediscovered in the 1940s, Williams produced his own tribute with the title "Ol Bunk's Band." Seeking the experience of music in words is, of course, a familiar literary exercise—words after the wordless. And Williams does capture something of the rhythmic urgency of jazz. But just as a musician of ordinary talent relies on routine phrases and harmonies, Williams invokes only popular and stereotypical ideas of jazz and its first artists: primitive, virile, at home in debauchery, and burdened by feelings of social injustice.

We may be tempted to find in Williams merely a historical curiosity. But only a few years ago an acclaimed study of the 1960s classified jazz as essentially part of the "hipster experience" and termed it "uninhibited black music." The author could do no better than quote this description of the motive for jazz from a popular magazine of the 1920s: ". . . an unloosing of instincts that nature wisely has taught us to hold in check, but which, every now and then, for cryptic reasons, are allowed to break the bonds of civilization."[2] The lack of everything but unintended irony suggests the great opportunity for developing a broader interpretive vocabulary and promoting historical and other forms of academic scholarship.

Hentoff's career conveniently represents at least the first such path, including close personal relations with the actual working world of jazz. But as the historian E. J. Hobsbawm noted recently, there is now a large and active "academic underground" of jazz scholars. Some are themselves musicians and write from that perspective. To be sure, Hobsbawm states unequivocally that "the jazz fan, however knowledgeable, is fundamentally a lover" and that even works of serious scholarship display the music as an "object of passion."[3] Yet, as we are discovering about inquiry across the disciplines, personal and group ideologies—the "social construction of knowledge" as it is sometimes called—have long been an important if unacknowledged part of many fields. Indeed, the metaphor of an "underground" for jazz studies is apt, suggesting those

qualities of devotion, partisanship, community, and inevitable fac-
tionalism, characteristic of oppositional political movements.

The diversity of jazz writing, in and around academic efforts,
represents the many interests brought to it. Historians, composers,
musicologists, ethnographers, archivists, collectors, discographers,
literary critics, journalists, practitioners of American Studies and
the various forms of ethnic studies, and indeed performers themselves, all undertake the work and usually with different goals in
mind. Accordingly, they disagree about what constitutes authority
in jazz research and criticism, about what kinds of knowledge and
experience are essential.[4]

Jazz writing is perhaps most familiar to general readers in
the performance or record review, though the lasting ones are typically occasions for a statement about the direction of a particular
career. Yet the more extended study of jazz periods, styles, and
performers is flourishing, as a recent bibliographic review makes
plain. Nonetheless, according to jazz historian William Howland
Kenney III, two key problems remain: reconciling the history of
music with the history of the varied contexts in which it is made
and used and establishing a workable approach to the demands
on a general audience of a specialized musical vocabulary.[5]

Even as efforts on behalf of synthesis gain momentum, jazz
writing continues to mingle points of view and purposes. It still
counts on strongly expressed personal engagement with the music
or well-known performers to carry observations about the origins,
structure, and functions of jazz.[6] The relation of jazz to the other
arts, and especially the status of improvisation in making and maintaining aesthetic principles is a compelling dilemma. By accepting
improvisation as an essential "flaw" one critic has proposed a definition of form that can account for jazz structure within the spontaneity of performance.[7] And as jazz continues to penetrate elite culture and mainstream popular culture—recent jazz films have
achieved great popularity in the intellectual community and Monk
tunes can now be heard in Muzak versions—partisans dispute not
only particulars of its standards of performance but also essentials
of fact and history.[8]

The relations between music and society may get no further
than occasions insisted upon by composers and the public attitudes of well-known musicians: Charles Mingus, for example, and
his "Fables of Faubus." On this question poet and professor Michael
Harper, known for the influence of jazz on his work and for his

own ideas on the role of jazz in racial identity and community, offers this comment: "Most great art is finally testamental: its technical brilliance never overshadows the content of the song: 'Deliver the melody, make sure the harmony's correct, play as long as you like, but play sweet, and don't forget the ladies.'"[9] Finally, to some writers the extramusical intentions of musicians and poets, critics and scholars, and debates about jazz history and other matters, may be beside the point; the "purity" of the music is the only element of jazz worth attention.[10]

As these examples and the bibliographic record of the past few decades suggest jazz writing will move only fitfully toward a general synthesis, and the problem of reaching a general audience in the vocabulary of the music itself will likely require its gradual addition to accessible forms of social or cultural history (hence Kenney's advice about doing it "gently"). As an object of study another source of jazz's appeal may be in the examples of independence and experimentation displayed by performers. Jazz scholars will be no less idiosyncratic, however much the routines of academic discourse impose superficial forms of orderliness. Indeed, more traditional fields of inquiry, like literary studies, can now be said to be experiencing versions of the problems cited by Kenney as typical of jazz scholarship. Nonetheless, the very choice of jazz as a subject identifies academic writers risking some professional marginality on behalf of their "passion." The struggle for the legitimacy of jazz has found new locations: the classroom and the library.

Today's jazz scholars are at work on aspects of the story: the origins, roles and fates of pioneering figures, the making and influence of performance and recording styles, and relations between music and other fields of expression or inquiry. But they are united in the belief that writing has an important role in jazz, one that complements Jo Jones's proposal that the only task is accounting for authenticity in performance.

Most essays in *Jazz In Mind* were initially presented at a scholarly conference at the University of Minnesota in fall 1987. Colleagues at the School of Music and the Department of Afro-American Studies, including Geneva Southall, Alex Lubet, Lloyd Ultan, Johannes Reidel, and John Wright have helped sustain jazz study at the university. Leslie Denny of the Department of Professional Development and Conference Services provided indispensable help in all aspects of the conference. Other department members, especially Trisha Tatam, also assisted as did Willard Jenkins, then jazz program director for Arts Midwest and Tom Trow of the university's College of Liberal Arts. Merry Jo Myhre saw the typing of the manuscript through several versions. We also had the help of Deborah Wolfangel in becoming better computer users. Ann Kirby assisted in other ways. Dean Harold Miller and Associate Dean Barbara Stuhler of Continuing Education and Extension also provided support, not the least of which was financial through CEE's Program Innovation Fund, for the conference and this book. Kathy Wildfong at the Wayne State University Press has been a patient and perceptive editor. Finally, the essays "James Reese Europe and the Prehistory of Jazz" by R. Reid Badger and "Jazz as Social Structure, Process and Outcome" by David T. Bastien and Todd J. Hostager have appeared in earlier versions respectively in *American Music* (Spring 1989) and *Communication Research* (December 1988). Material is reprinted here by permission.

Notes

1. Nat Hentoff, *Boston Boy: A Memoir* (Boston: Faber and Faber, 1987), 121.

2. Allen J. Matusow, *The Unravelling of America: A History of Liberalism in the 1960s* (New York: Harper and Row, 1984), 280–81.

3. E. J. Hobsbawm, "The Jazz Comeback." *New York Review of Books*, February 12, 1987, p. 11.

4. Lewis Porter, "Problems in Jazz Research," *Black Music Research Journal* 8 (Fall 1988): 1–13.

5. William Howland Kenney III, "Jazz: A Bibliographic Essay," *American Studies International* 25 (April 1987): 4.

6. Gerald Early, "The Passing of Jazz's Old Guard: Remembering Charles Mingus, Thelonious Monk, and Sonny Stitt." *Kenyon Review*, n.s. 7 (Spring 1985): 21–36.

7. Red Gioia, "The Aesthetics of Imperfection," *Hudson Review* 30 (Winter 1987): 585–600.

8. A good place to observe recent controversies is in the political and literary journal *The New Republic*. See James Lincoln Collier's "The Faking of Jazz" on the ideological meaning of the jazz expatriates phenomenon (November 18, 1985) and Stanley Crouch's "Bird Land" on the authenticity of Clint Eastwood's film *Bird* (February 27, 1989).

9. Michael S. Harper, "Don't they speak jazz?" *Triquarterly* 55 (Fall 1982): 179.

10. Hayden Carruth, "The Formal Idea of Jazz," in *In Praise of What Persists*, ed. Stephen Berg (New York: Harper and Row, 1983), 24–32. The matter of representing jazz in fiction suggests how powerful the impure approach remains. Toni Morrison's *The Bluest Eye* (1970) introduces a long passage of psychological analysis with some regret about the limits of words in relation to jazz: "The pieces of Cholly's life could become coherent only in the head of a musician. Only those who talk their talk through the gold of curved metal, or in the touch of black-and-white rectangles and taut skins and strings echoing from wooden corridors, could give true form to his life."

JAMES REESE EUROPE
and the
PREHISTORY OF JAZZ

R. Reid Badger

On May 10, 1919, some seven months before America's Jazz Age was officially ushered in, the front page of the *New York World* announced that James Reese Europe, the "King of Jazz Music," had been tragically killed during a performance of his band at Boston's Mechanics Hall.[1] At the time of his death, thirty-eight year old Jim Europe had already achieved a remarkable position in American popular music. A prolific composer of popular songs, dance tunes, marches, and ragtime, Europe was also prominent in the emerging black musical theater in New York, and, in 1912, led the first orchestra of black musicians to appear at Carnegie Hall. As a principal supplier of dance orchestras to New York's social elite and accompanist to Vernon and Irene Castle with his own "society orchestra," he was a central figure in the dance craze that swept the country in the years prior to World War I. During the war, he led the celebrated 369th Infantry "Hellfighters" Band of the American Expeditionary Force, which some have claimed first introduced France to American syncopated music, and at the time of his death Europe was the best known black band leader in America.

Europe's short career obviously touches upon a number of important issues in the evolution of American popular music and the transformation of American musical taste in the first decades of this century. The purpose of this essay, however, is to consider only one aspect of that career—his relationship and that of his music to the actual development of jazz during the period prior to 1920 where few recordings (the basic historical source for jazz) are available. In 1919, "jazz" was a very imprecise term compared to current definitions, or indeed even to the popular understanding that emerged during the 1920s. Nevertheless, between roughly 1908 and 1919 certain subtle modifications of popular ragtime-based rhythms and tonality, along with an increasing acceptance of extemporization, gained such widespread recognition that by the latter date it was common in the United States and Europe to speak of the existence of a new music; that music was called jazz. Coinciding with these critical formative years, Jim Europe's career and his music provide important insights into the emergence and diffusion of the new music and suggest the generally unappreciated role that more formally educated black musicians played in that process.

Europe's early musical training began at home with the piano and violin and included studies in composition with Enrico Hulei of the Marine Corps Band as well as other notable musicians and teachers living in Washington, D.C.[2] In 1903, following the death of his father, he moved to New York hoping to secure a place for himself as writer or musical director of one of the black Broadway shows that had become increasingly popular in those years. Following a year as a cabaret pianist, he was asked by Ernest Hogan, a pioneering Broadway performer and businessman, to help write the music for a variety show he was organizing. Hogan's group of some twenty or so musicians, singers, and dancers—billed as the "Memphis Students"—were such a resounding hit at Hammerstein's Victoria Theater that they were held over for five months. Although James Weldon Johnson later described them as "the first jazz band ever heard on a New York stage," the strictly musical significance of the group is probably limited to the novel inclusion of a saxophone in an orchestra consisting principally of banjos, mandolins, and guitars (instruments then associated with folk music or minstrelsy), to the energetic and acrobatic drumming of Buddy Gilmore, and to the impromptu dancing of Will Dixon.[3] Their material consisted primarily of orchestrated instrumental ragtime and syncopated versions of popular songs, but they also are known to have featured more ambitious pieces like Will Marion Cook's *Swing Along*.[4]

Europe's stint with the Memphis Students was followed by a succession of successful appointments as writer and musical director for many leading musical comedies of the next five years, among them Cole and Johnson's "Shoo-Fly Regiment" (1906–7) and "Red Moon" (1908–9), and Bert Williams's "Mr. Lode of Koal" (1909–10).[5] These were exciting years for black musical comedy, promising greater freedom for black entertainers and musicians to include more honestly Afro-American material in their shows. For Europe, his six years on the road provided invaluable musical experience and training and reinforced his growing conviction that a distinctive Afro-American artistic idiom was awaiting development.[6] By the spring of 1910, he had achieved a reputation as one of the major composers and directors in black musical theater. Unfortunately, the almost simultaneous loss of Hogan, George Walker, and Bob Cole, coupled with the cooling in white acceptance of black entertainers, initiated a period of "almost total exodus of black performers from the mainstream theaters of New York."[7]

Dance orchestras remained popular in the hotels and cabarets, however, and while black musicians found sporadic employment in the then fashionable "gypsy ensembles," there was a definite lack of organization, and jobs in the better paying downtown locations were rare. Realizing that if black musicians were going to prosper and their music was to develop they would need to organize themselves more systematically, on April 11, 1910, Europe and several other established black composers and players—including Will Vodery, William Tyers, Ford Dabney, and Joe Jordan—formed the Clef Club. The purpose of the club was to provide a central union, clearinghouse, and booking agency for the employment of black musicians anywhere in New York and to oversee their contracts and guarantee their professionalism. By fronting its own highly publicized orchestra consisting of its best musicians, the club also sought to secure the black musician's place in the forefront of the public's mind.[8]

Jim Europe was elected both president of the organization and conductor of the Clef Club Orchestra which gave its first performance on May 27, 1910, at Harlem's Manhattan Casino. Europe kept the program simple (light classics, a concert waltz, Joe Jordan's *That Teasing Rag*, and his own *Clef Club March*), and the hundred-

21

member orchestra was so well received that other concerts followed in regular succession.[9] His crowning achievement with the orchestra occurred on May 2, 1912, when he brought them to the stage of Carnegie Hall for a "symphony" of "Negro music." It would be hard to overestimate the significance of the event; twelve years before the Paul Whiteman-George Gershwin concert at the Aeolian Hall and twenty-six years before the Benny Goodman concert of 1938, Europe had "stormed the bastion of the white musical establishment and made many members of New York's cultural elite aware of Negro music for the first time."[10] So well-received was the concert, that the Clef Club Orchestra returned to Carnegie Hall for performances in 1913 and 1914.[11]

There are no recorded performances of the large Clef Club Orchestra, but from programs and reviews of the concerts it is known that Europe employed great sections of mandolins, banjos or bandolas, and harp guitars, as well as strings, brass, woodwinds, pianos, and percussion. The music Europe composed and arranged for the orchestra included marches, rags, current popular tunes and musical theater pieces, and classical themes—the sort of material that the public expected from concert bands like John Phillip Sousa's, but he increasingly featured compositions by black composers and adaptations of the traditional spirituals. Europe admitted that he was forced to modify the usual instrumentation (two clarinets in place of an oboe, baritone horns in place of French horns, trombones substituting for bassoons) at first because he was simply unable to find capable black performers. As he moved the orchestra toward playing Afro-American music exclusively, he became more convinced of the appropriateness of the sound he had created.[12]

In an interview with the *New York Evening Post* in March 1914, Europe explained that he did not wish to attempt to imitate the methods and organization of a white orchestra, but rather to develop "a kind of symphony music that, no matter what else you may think, is different and distinctive, and that lends itself to the playing of the peculiar compositions of our race."[13] The most unusual and noticeable aspect of the orchestral sound was its "very imposing and seductively rhythmic" character, which was underscored by large batteries of drums, timpani, and traps.[14] "Although we have first violins," he explained, "the place of the second violins with us is taken by mandolins and banjos. This gives that peculiar steady strumming accompaniment to our music which all people comment on, and which is something like that of the Russian Bala-laika Orchestra, I believe. Then, for background, we employ ten pianos. That, in itself, is sufficient to amuse the average white musi-cian who attends one of our concerts for the first time. The result, however, is a background of chords which are essentially typical of negro [sic] harmony."[15]

As novel or dramatic as the public performances of the or-chestra were, or as ambitious as he was to establish "an orchestra of Negroes which will be able to take its place among the serious musical organizations of the country," Europe also realized the practical importance to black musicians of taking advantage of the increasing vogue of black performers in the field of popular enter-tainment. Between 1910 and 1914, in fact, Europe's Clef Club was the greatest force for organizing and channeling the efforts of black musicians in New York, providing musicians for vaudeville orches-tras, hotel bands, and increasingly, for private society dances. It was natural for the black musician to take the lead in providing popular music, especially to accompany the new "modern" dance steps, he said, because "they were all danced and played by Negroes long before the whites took them up."[16]

By the summer of 1913, Europe himself was directing the Clef Club's "Exclusive Society Orchestra" for the Astors, Vanderbilts, and other members of New York's elite.[17] About this time he began his partnership with the legendary dancing team of Vernon and Irene Castle.[18] As Irene remembered it, they wanted Jim Europe's orches-tra not only because it was the most famous one of its kind but also, she said, because Europe "was a skilled musician and one of the first to take jazz out of the saloons and make it respectable. All the men in his orchestra could read music, a rarity in those days."[19] According to Eubie Blake, who, along with Noble Sissle, joined Europe in the spring of 1916, "that Europe gang were abso-lute reading sharks. They could read a moving snake and if a fly lit on that paper he got played."[20]

Beginning on opening night at the Castle House, New York's elite learned to stumble through the tango and maxixe to the music of Europe's eleven-piece Society Orchestra and to brave such origi-nal steps as the half-and-half, the innovation, and the foxtrot. Eu-rope and Vernon Castle conceived the latter, the most famous of the Castle dances, after an initial suggestion by W. C. Handy.[21] By early 1914, the Castles' dances had become so fashionable in New York that in April of that year a tour of thirty-two major American and Canadian cities was arranged, and the entire company went on the road for a whirlwind twenty-eight days.

Later that same year the Victor Company offered Europe a recording contract, one of the first given to a Negro musician and the first ever to a black orchestra. He was now such an important figure in the New York entertainment world that a *New York Herald* reporter, sent to interview him, declared that "Europe's orchestra . . . has all but secured complete control of the cabaret and dance field in the city." Europe agreed, "Our Negro orchestras have nearly cleared the field."[22]

There is fairly good evidence of the music Europe performed with the smaller Clef Club "Society Orchestra" which became so popular for New York social dancing during his association with the Castles. The instrumentation for these groups, which ranged from six to a dozen pieces, consisted of a pair of violins, a clarinet and cornet playing the melody (usually in unison), and two banjos or mandolins, a trombone, piano, string bass, and drums providing harmonic and rhythmic accompaniment. Sometimes a cello, a baritone, or a flute was added, and there are reports (but no recordings) of an occasional saxophone. Because the society orchestras were dance bands, they tended to concentrate on popular material, some of which was written by Europe and the rest arranged by him, but the distinctive sound they produced seems to have been the result of a looser or freer approach to tonal variation and interpretation by the performers. Drums and syncopated rhythms were still prominent, but "the way the men handled their instruments, and the way they produced their tones" was new.[23] A typical piece would be composed of perhaps a half-dozen melodic strains "which were repeated until the leader felt that the dancers were near exhaustion," and the end would be signaled by a sudden increase in volume, acceleration in tempo, and greater emphasis on the rhythm section.[24] "We would run down new arrangements right on the stand with people dancing," Blake recalled, "and they wouldn't even know it."[25]

For the first Victor recordings of the Society Orchestra, made on December 29, 1913, Europe used a fairly large group of fourteen pieces, including five mandolins or banjos. Of the four sides cut that day, two were one-steps or turkey trots (*Tres Moutarde*, very roughly translated as *Too Much Mustard*, a popular tune by the Englishman Cecil Macklin, and *Down Home Rag*, by bandleader Wilber Sweatman), one was a tango (*El Irresistable*), and one a

24

maxixe (*Amapa*). The first two pieces, written in 2/4 time, but taken at a fast tempo, display an unmistakable rhythmic vitality and excitement, and, despite the simple and repetitious melodies, one is forced to agree with Gunther Schuller that they "must have been electrifying to dance to."[26]

It is interesting to compare the Europe version of *Down Home Rag*, his first record, with that recorded by the Six Brown Brothers, a popular white saxophone sextet, eighteen months later.[27] In both performances the four strain form of the piece (AABBAACCDDCC) is faithfully followed, though Europe added a short intro and a tag ending, and there is little textural variation among the strains. All the instruments play the melodies virtually all the time, either harmonized or in unison, in a clearly vertical fashion. Despite these similarities, the two interpretations of *Down Home* could hardly be more different. The Brown Brothers' performance, taken at an unbelievably slow tempo, is so stiff and mechanical as to be almost comical. There is a certain competence but no momentum, no rhythmic vitality, and no tonal variety. Except for the possibly novel sound of the saxophone family itself, it is difficult to understand the appeal of such a record; it certainly doesn't seem to point in any new directions. The Europe Orchestra's reading, however, is exuberant. Not only is the piece played very fast—twice the tempo of the Brown version, but the emotional intensity of the performance infects even the performers themselves, who seem unable to resist joining the drum and cymbal punctuations with their ad-lib vocal shouts and laughter. Although things never get out of control and the band follows the score, there is a clear sense in this early Europe recording that interpretation is of at least equal value to composition; that how something is played is as important as what is played, especially if that something is intended for dancing. The additional Victor recordings cut early the following February are more directly associated with the Castles and even more revealing.

The second session, for which Europe dispensed with the banjo/mandolins and added a flute, included a waltz, a popular tune, *You're Here and I'm Here*, and two Europe originals, *Castle House Rag* and *Castle Walk*. *You're Here* is of interest chiefly because it was one of two songs written by Jerome Kern in 1914 (the other being *They Didn't Believe Me*) which mark a crucial turning point in his young career away from the European operetta and toward a more native style.[28] Europe's treatment of Kern's syncopated melody is straightforward and danceable, though in the contrasting wood blocks and snare drums there is more than a suggestion of 4/4 time (rather than the 2/4 of the original sheet music). All the recordings made at the February 1914 session are in fact slower and less frenetic than *Tres Moutarde* or especially *Down Home Rag*, and they may, as Lawrence Gushee has argued, "presage the turn from the one-step and turkey trot to the foxtrot."[29] They may also be among the first recorded evidence of the impact of the blues.

Europe did not record a true blues until 1919 when he recorded both *Memphis Blues* and *Saint Louis Blues*, but he had been performing them with the Castles as early as 1913 and was, according to composer W. C. Handy, the first to play *Memphis Blues*.[30] In the November 1914 *Tribune* interview, Europe described *Memphis* as a dance—the foxtrot, one which Vernon Castle did not at first think suitable because the time was "too slow, the world of today demanding staccato music." Eventually, however, Europe recalled, "he began to dance it at private entertainments in New York, and, to his astonishment, discovered that it was immediately taken up. It was not until then that Mr. and Mrs. Castle began to dance it in public, with the result that it is now danced as much as all the other dances put together."[31] As Europe saw it, the newer dances that were replacing the turkey trots and other ragtime dances were more directly rooted in the Afro-American tradition.

Of the specific pieces recorded that day, *Castle House Rag* is something of a small revelation and therefore deserves closer attention. The form of the piece follows that of Scott Joplin's classic (and commercially successful) *Maple Leaf Rag* in that it consists of four melodic strains played in an AABBACCDD pattern. The first strain, employing fast sixteenth notes and shifting between minor and major keys, suggests several ragtime melodic and rhythmic ideas; the second section seems more related to march music, although it is quieter and dominated by the violins; and the third is a stop-time trio using contrasting instrumentation common to both orchestral ragtime and march music, and the drums lay out. The fourth strain, however, is quite different, exhibiting a less formal and more relaxed approach, as if the musicians unexpectedly abandoned the written score and, following Cricket Smith's cornet lead and the increasing domination of Buddy Gilmore's drum breaks, improvised a ferociously wild climax.[32] "With half a minute of recording time left," suggests Gushee, "Europe may have let his band loose for three choruses of ad-hoc basic rag, accidentally transmitting to us the only example from its time of orchestral ragtime extemporization."[33]

Europe's success continued throughout 1915. It was his most active year with the Castles, and he played with them everywhere —in dance halls, cabarets, private homes, on tour, and even on film. Although the team had made dancing virtually a national pastime, it is difficult to see how much further their collaboration might have carried them if World War I had not dramatically intervened in their lives. In December, with his native Britain locked in a war of attrition with Germany, Vernon Castle enlisted in the Royal Air Force, and nine months later Jim Europe joined New York's Negro regiment, the Fifteenth Infantry of the National Guard. Commissioned as a line officer, one of a handful of black officers even in the segregated black regiments, he was initially assigned to a machine-gun company. The Fifteenth's commanding officer, Colonel William Hayward, however, in an effort to boost enlistments, prevailed upon Europe to organize a regimental brass band. At the time, Europe was not particularly interested in military bands, but he recognized that they were becoming increasingly popular as the United States edged closer to war, and he also became convinced that if he formed a really first-rate band, then he would have no trouble later in getting support for a Negro symphony orchestra and for the black Broadway musical production he truly wanted.[34]

Although it was not easy to convince the kind of professional musicians Europe wanted to quit their civilian jobs and enlist in the army in wartime, by the end of May 1917 he had recruited some forty musicians including Eugene Mikell, an instructor of bands and a fine cornet and saxophone player, and Frank DeBroite, one of the premier black cornet soloists in the country.[35] The first public performance of the new Fifteenth Regimental Band took place in late June at the Manhattan Casino where a very large crowd (perhaps as many as four thousand) gathered to hear what the society dance orchestra leader could do with a military ensemble.[36] Virtually all the band's rehearsal time had been spent on the concert music that Europe had prepared for the first part of the evening's program. According to Sissle, who was the regiment's drum major, the band played the concert marches and overtures quite well considering the short period they had been together. But the climax of the affair came "when the attendants began clearing away the chairs and sprinkling powder over the hard wood" in preparation for the dance portion of the program. It hardly seemed to matter that the dance pieces had barely been rehearsed; "Jim was there with his baton and everyone of those musicians was 'raring to go. The crowd was no more anxious to hear them play some jazz than they were to play it. . . . I will never forget the yell that went up after Jim had conducted the first dance number. What we thought was a wonderful demonstration of appreciation after each concert number, turned out to be but a ripple on the ocean compared with that mighty roar that followed the last strain of the first jazz tune."[37] Typical of the dance pieces that, from that first performance, received the greatest public response were Europe's arrangements of the blues. The *Army Blues* and Handy's *Memphis Blues* became two of the band's specialities.

In July, New York's Fifteenth Regiment was mustered into federal service, and, following six months of training, on New Year's Day, 1918, they marched ashore at Brest, France, as an official unit of the American Expeditionary Force. Shortly thereafter orders were received to have the band—its fame and that of its leader having preceded them—detached for the entertainment of the first U.S. soldiers on leave at Aix-les-Bains. Between February 12 and March 17, 1918, the Fifteenth Regimental Band traveled more than two thousand miles, performing for French, British, and American troops and for French civilians in some twenty-five cities. Sissle's colorful description of the band's first concert before an entirely French audience in the town of Tours gives a fair idea of the kind of music they performed and the positive reception they received throughout their year in France. The program began with a French march, followed by familiar overtures and vocal selections, "all of which were heartily applauded." The second part of the program opened with Sousa's *Stars and Stripes Forever* and "before the last note of the martial ending had been finished the house was ringing with applause." Next followed an arrangement of Southern, or "plantation melodies" and then came "the fireworks, 'The Memphis Blues.'" Following Europe's example, the musicians relaxed their stiff military demeanor, half closed their eyes, and as the baton came down with a "soul-rousing crash" of cymbals, "both director and musicians seemed to forget their surroundings." "Cornet and clarinet players began to manipulate notes in that typical rhythm (that rhythm which no artist has ever been able to put down on paper)," the drummers hit their stride with shoulders shaking in syncopated time, and Europe turned to the trombones "who sat patiently waiting for their cue to have a 'jazz spasm.'" "The audience could stand it no longer, the 'jazz germ' hit them and it seemed to find the vital spot loosening all muscles and causing what is known in America as an 'eagle rocking it.'" There now, Sissle said to himself, "'Colonel Hayward has brought his band over here and started ragtimitis in France; ain't this an awful thing to visit upon a nation with so many burdens?' But when the band had finished and the people were roaring with laughter, their faces wreathed in smiles, I was forced to say that this is just what France needs at this critical time."[38] Virtually everywhere they played during the tour, New York's Fifteenth Regimental Band was enthusiastically, sometimes even wildly, received, and the reports of their success spread throughout the expeditionary force and to the papers back home.

On March 14, 1918, Europe and his fellow musicians were directed to rejoin their regiment, which had since been renamed the 369th U.S. Infantry Regiment and assigned as such to the Sixteenth Division of the French Army at the front near Givry-en-Argonne. Jim Europe took great pride in the fact that the men of his band served as not only entertainers but also combat soldiers who fought alongside their comrades in the trenches for nearly four months of the Great War.[39] Prior to this time, the American Fifteenth Regiment's reputation rested primarily on the fame of its band and its celebrated leader. During the summer and fall of 1918, however, the new 369th distinguished itself as a courageous and effective fighting outfit, earning the nickname of the "Hellfighters" for its exploits and emerging after the Allied victory in November as one of the most highly decorated American units of the war.

Lt. Europe and the "Hellfighters" band were not with their regiment during the final push to the Rhine and victory, however. With the tide of battle beginning to turn in the Allies' favor, Colonel Hayward finally acceded to a French request that the band be sent to Paris for a single concert. Europe protested that he had not conducted the band since spring, but in the end he went and their performance was received with such unrestrained enthusiasm that the French officials insisted they remain for eight additional weeks. The climax came with a concert at the Tuileries Gardens where, along with the British Grenadiers, the Garde Republicane, and the Royal Italian bands, they played before a crowd estimated at fifty

thousand. Although the "Hellfighters" could not compete techni-
cally with the other great military bands, they nevertheless won
the crowd over completely. Europe's explanation, given to *New York
Tribune* correspondant Grenville Vernon, is revealing:

> After the concert was over the leader of the band of the Garde
> Republicain [sic] came over and asked me for the score of one
> of the jazz compositions we had played. He said he wanted
> his band to play it. I gave it to him, and the next day he again
> came to see me. He explained that he couldn't seem to get
> the effects I got, and asked me to go to a rehearsal. I went
> with him. The great band played the composition superbly
> —but he was right: the jazz effects were missing. I took an
> instrument and showed him how it could be done, and he
> told me that his own musicians felt sure that my band had
> used special instruments. Indeed, some of them, afterward at-
> tending one of my rehearsals, did not believe what I had said
> until after they had examined the instruments used by my
> men.[40]

Having rejoined their unit, Lt. Europe and the "Jazziest, crazi-
est, best tooting outfit in France" gave their last concert on the
evening of January 31; early the next morning they were on their
way home.[41] On February 17, 1919, the Fifteenth National Guard
Regiment of New York, known in France as the 369th United States
Infantry, marched up Fifth Avenue to the cheers of a million New
Yorkers and on to Harlem to be received by their friends and loved
ones with a frenzy of pride and joy. A month after their triumphant
return, Europe and his much expanded "Hellfighters" band embarked upon a worldwide tour with two concerts in Manhatten.
An exclusive recording contract was announced by Pathe Record
Company for the "Jazz King" and his "famous overseas band," and
the first recordings began to appear by the end of April.[42]

It seems clear that in his direction of the "Hellfighters" Jim
Europe still maintained a fairly tight rein on his players and continued to insist that they read accurately and execute with clean intonation and precise pitch when he wanted it. There is ample evidence, however, that he also—when the band performed its most
uninhibited rhythmic numbers—encouraged the use of mutes, various unusual tonguing techniques, and even permitted occasional
ad-libbed solos.[43] The *New York Sun*, in its review of the band's
concert at the Manhattan Opera House on March 16, 1919, de-

scribed the performance as "a flood of good music, a gorgeous racket of syncopation and jazzing, extraordinary-pleasing violin and cornet solos and many other features that bands seldom offer."[44]

Four recording sessions for Pathe between March 3 and May 7, produced some twenty-four sides, including several songs by Noble Sissle and Creighton Thompson and a number of popular tunes like *Ja Da* and *Darktown Strutters' Ball*. Not surprisingly, the strictly instrumental numbers provide the most evidence for what might be best described as jazz interpretation—those slight alterations (smears, slurs, rhythmic or dynamic shifts), occasional "blue" notes, tonal coloration (use of mutes), and improvised or paraphrased breaks. Much of the material is uneven, but, as Schuller has said, in a "real sense this was the first big band. Naturally the pieces had to be arranged. To hear a whole clarinet section take a clamorous break, as on *That's Got Em* or *Clarinet Marmelade*, is to recapture, I am sure, some of the wild abandon of the early New Orleans marching bands."[45] Compared to the white concert bands of the time, who "could take a ragtime or early jazz piece and make it stiff and polite," Jim Europe's band "could take a polite salon piece and make it swing—in a rudimentary sort of way."[46] Of particular interest are the band's recordings of two pieces written by W. C. Handy: *St. Louis Blues* and *Memphis Blues*. As Charles Hamm has noted, most blues published and recorded before the mid-twenties bear little resemblance to the formal and harmonic patterns of traditional vocal blues and at most may contain only a twelve-bar blues phrase or two "embedded in a larger structure."[47] *Memphis Blues* is such a piece. Europe's recording begins with a short introduction followed by a twelve-measure blues phrase and then a sixteen-measure section similar to ragtime. The final section consists of another twelve-bar blues played six times, each featuring a different instrumentalist whose short solo is "surely not written into the score Europe had prepared for the band" and which may constitute the first swinging jazz breaks on record.[48] Europe referred to these blues pieces as foxtrots, and he had been playing them ever since his days with the Castles. The significant thing about the foxtrot was that, although the name suggests a kinship with the other ragtime animal dances like the turkey trot, it actually represents a "radical slowing down of the accompanying music" and a turning away from the increasingly speeded-up 2/4 staccato of ragtime.[49] In Jim Europe's recordings one can hear this critical rhythmic shift that necessarily preceeded the emergence of the classic blues-based jazz of the 1920s.

As Europe and the "Hellfighters" began their tour in the spring of 1919, they were greeted by enthusiastic crowds in every city they visited, and the press remarked on the leader's warmth and geneality. Then suddenly and tragically Jim Europe's career was over. During a performance in Boston on May 9, he was fatally stabbed by a mentally disturbed member of the band and died within a few hours. The entire country was dismayed and shocked by the tragedy. Funeral services, held at St. Mark's in New York on May 13, were attended by a throng of the prominent and the less so, and people wept openly as his bier was carried slowly through the streets of Harlem. Following a second service in Washington, D.C., the following day, he was buried with full military honors in Arlington National Cemetery.[50]

It is tempting to speculate upon what further contributions Jim Europe might have made had he lived; clearly, he was not one to rest on his achievements, and he most certainly would be better known today. Europe's reputation has suffered because he was a true transitional figure and, like other transitional figures, has unfortunately been difficult to place. While he was steadfastly committed to increasing the respect accorded Afro-American music and to improving conditions for black Americans, he seems to have remained apart, at least politically, from direct involvement in the racial ferment of the times. His association with the Castles and with the white musical and social establishment of New York has also tended to make his position in Afro-American history somewhat ambiguous. In addition, Europe's private life and personal habits, unlike those of so many other more flamboyant entertainers of the period, were never the sensational stuff that makes for good copy; in fact, surprisingly little is actually known of his personal or family life.

Historians of "serious" American music have seen Europe as a mere band leader, an accomplished one, perhaps, but essentially a popularizer rather than an innovator. Popular culture historians and folklore specialists have, for their part, found him too stiff in his demeanor, too formally educated, or too commercially successful to qualify for inclusion within the ranks of their humble and untutored heroes. More unfortunate still has been the lack of attention given Europe by scholars and writers who, in their efforts to

establish the unique artistic qualities of American jazz, have con-
centrated upon the Mortons and the Olivers and have tended to
dismiss Europe's electic music as having only a tangential relationship to their subject. His relatively few recordings do seem on first
hearing to have little to do with the small-group Dixieland style
jazz generally assumed to be the first fully realized expression of
the music. In addition, Europe's musical achievement lies primarily
in orchestration and arrangement, rather than individual performance, the hallmark of small-group jazz.

When considering the roots of early jazz, however, it is important to remember that we have an imprecise and incomplete sense
of how the music sounded prior to 1920. Without denigrating the
important contributions of those justly celebrated pionee vho
provided the classic recordings of that latter decade, it seems rea-
sonable to apply a somewhat broader and more generous definition
in assessing the musical achievement of those more formally educated individuals like Europe. One potential benefit is that we
may discover a wider pattern in the evolutionary lines that lead
in important, and perhaps even critical, ways to the emergence
and certainly the diffusion of jazz.[51] Moreover, by recognizing
the achievement of Jim Europe, one is better able to understand
the musical and historical context that eventually produced such
major jazz orchestrators as Fletcher Henderson and Duke
Ellington.

If for no reasons other than his influence on countless musicians of the Jazz Age and his leadership in the Clef Club, Jim Europe
should be recognized as a significant contributor to Afro-American
music in general and jazz in particular. Before he arrived in New
York, jazz was a little-known word, and if known at all, it was probably a vulgarity; by the time of his death it had become an accepted,
if not entirely acceptable, term for describing a musical revolution.
As much as anyone, Jim Europe, an articulate musician and war
hero, was responsible for making the term and music widely respectable not only at home in America but also in England and
on the continent. As the first black band leader to be offered a
major recording contract, he opened an essential door for jazz
without which the future development of the music would be in-
conceivable. For these, as well as for his more strictly musical contributions, James Reese Europe deserves a place alongside Jelly
Roll Morton as one of the most important individuals in the prehistory of jazz.

Notes

Research support for this article was provided by the National Endowment for the Humanities, Summer Seminars Program, and the Research Grants Committee of the University of Alabama. The author also wishes to thank James Reese Europe, Jr., for his assistance.

1. *New York World*, Sunday, May 11, 1919. In an editorial the following day, the newspaper went even further, calling him "the originator of jazz music."

2. "Men of the Month," *The Crisis*, June 1912, 67–68. He may have also been a student of Joseph Douglass and Hans Hanke, of the Leipzig Conservatory. Later, in New York, he did study with Harry T. Burleigh and Melville Charlton. The Europe family was musical; James's mother, Lorraine, played piano regularly in the Baptist Church, and young Europe, his sister Mary, and an older brother John, each demonstrated an early musical aptitude. Mary, three years James's junior, was educated at Howard University and Columbia University Teachers College and for many years taught music in the Washington, D.C., high schools. She also toured for a time with the famous Coleridge-Taylor Choral Society of Washington, D.C., as its pianist. See Doris E. McGinty, "Gifted Minds and Pure Hearts: Mary L. Europe and Estelle Pinckney Webster," *The Journal of Negro Education* 51 (Summer 1982): 266–77. James's older brother, John, was the regular piano player at Barron Wilkins's Little Savoy Club in New York during the early 1910s, and Willie "the Lion" Smith recalls hearing him in Harlem about 1916. See *Music on My Mind* (New York: Doubleday, 1964) 55, 65.

3. James Weldon Johnson, *Black Manhatten* (New York: Alfred A. Knopf, 1930), 120. See also "Interview with Ernest Hogan," in *New York Age*, August 24, 1905, p. 7.

4. *New York Age*, May 6, 1915, p. 6, and October 26, 1905, p. 1.

5. See Samuel B. Charters and Leonard Kunstadt, *Jazz: A History of the New York Scene* (Garden City: Doubleday, 1962), 24, and Henry T. Sampson, *Blacks in Blackface: A Sourcebook on Early Black Musical Shows* (Metuchen, N.J.: Scarecrow Press, 1980), 148, 287, 362. The *New York Age*, Harlem's weekly newspaper, provided regular coverage of black musical theater activities during this period, and Europe is often mentioned. See, for example, *New York Age*, July 26, 1906, p. 6, and April 8, 1909, p. 6.

6. See James Reese Europe, "Negro's Place in Music," *New York Evening Post*, March 13, 1914; reprinted in Robert Kimball and William Bolcom, *Reminiscing with Sissle and Blake* (New York: Viking, 1973), 60–61.

7. See Kimball's excellent discussion in his liner notes for *Shuffle Along*, New World 260, in *The Recorded Anthology of American Music* (New York: New World Records, 1976), 1–2. See also Lester A. Walton, "Retirement of Cole and Johnson," in *New York Age*, July 14, 1910, p. 6.

8. See Charters and Kunstadt, 25–30; Johnson, 122–23, Smith, 62; and Terry Waldo, *This Is Ragtime* (New York: Hawthorn Books, 1976), 100.

9. See especially Lester A. Walton's review in the *New York Age*, June 2, 1910, p. 6, and Lucien H. White, "An Enjoyable Program," in *New York Age*, November 20, 1913, p. 6, which is quoted in Charters and Kunstadt, 32.

10. Gunther Schuller, "Europe, James Reese (1881–1919)," in Rayford W. Logan and Michael R. Winston, *Dictionary of American Negro Biography* (New York: W. W. Norton, 1982), 214. "Paul Whiteman," recalled Eubie Blake, "was not the first man that put jazz into Carnegie Hall. It was James Reese Europe." Quoted in Kimball and Bolcom, 239.

11. "In Retrospect: Black-Music Concerts in Carnegie Hall, 1912–1915," in *Black Perspective in Music* 6 (1978): 71–88, provides a useful reprint of six reviews of the Clef Club concerts.

12. Europe, "Negro's Place," 61.

13. Ibid.

14. David Mannes, *Music is My Faith* (New York: W. W. Norton, 1938), 218. Mannes, a New York concert violinist and music educator, was a friend and associate of Europe's in the establishment of a Music School Settlement project in Harlem. He personally attended several Clef Club Orchestra rehearsals and performances.

15. Europe, "Negro's Place," 61.

16. James Reese Europe, "Negro Composer on Race's Music," *New York Tribune*, November 22, 1914, and reprinted in *New York Age*, November 26, 1914, and in Kimball and Bolcom, 64.

17. See Lester A. Walton, "Musicians Play for 400," *New York Age*, September 4, 1913, p. 6.

18. There is a wealth of information about the Castles, who deserve treatment on their own, and their relationship with Europe. See, for example, Lewis A. Erenberg, *Steppin' Out: New York Nightlife and the Transformation of American Culture, 1890–1930* (Chicago: University of Chicago Press, 1981), 146–71; Charters and Kunstadt, 33–41; Schuller, "Europe," 214, Charles Hamm, *Yesterdays: Popular Music in America* (New York: W. W. Norton, 1979), 379; David L. Lewis, *When Harlem Was in Vogue* (New York: Knopf, 1981), 32–33; and Vernon and Irene Castle, *Modern Dancing* (New York: Harper, 1914), 17.

19. Irene Castle, *Castles in the Air* (Garden City: Doubleday, 1958), 92.

20. "Interview with Eubie Blake," in Rudi Blesh, *Combo USA: Eight Lives in Jazz* (Philadelphia: Chilton Book Company, 1971), 205.

21. Irene Castle to Noble Sissle, January 12, 1920, in Noble Lee Sissle, "Memoirs of Lieutenant 'Jim' Europe," NAACP Records 1940–55, Library of Congress, Group II, J Box 56, 25. This recently discovered 246-page manu-

script contains Sissle's personal memoirs of his association (1916–19) with Europe. It is especially valuable on their experience in World War I. See also Europe, "Negro Composer," 64; Charters and Kunstadt, 354–57; and Lewis, 32.

22. Quoted in Charters and Kunstadt, 41.

23. Eileen Southern, *The Music of Black Americans*, 2d ed. (New York: W. W. Norton, 1983), 345. See also Walton, "An Unusual Bill," *New York Age*, August 14, 1913; and Blesh, 205.

24. Gunther Schuller, *Early Jazz: Its Roots and Musical Development* (New York: Oxford University Press, 1968), 248. Schuller is the first modern writer to suggest that the strictly musical aspects of Europe's career deserve serious attention. His classic study, therefore, remains the best place to begin.

25. Quoted in Blesh, 205.

26. Schuller, *Early Jazz*, 248. The basic discographical information, included as an appendix to this book, was compiled from record labels, record company recording books and announcements, newspapers, and from the information contained in Brian Rust, *Jazz Records, 1897–1942* (New Rochelle: Arlington House, 1978), 512–13; *Record Research* 1 (December 1955); 3–5; Michael Montgomery, "Exploratory Discography of Noble Sissle, Eubie Blake, and James Reese Europe" in Kimball and Bolcom, 247–54; and Max Harrison, Charles Fox, and Eric Thacker, *The Essential Jazz Records: Vol. I, Ragtime to Swing* (Westport, Conn. Greenwood Press, 1984), 19–20.

27. A reissue of the Brown Brothers' recording can be found on *Steppin' on the Gas: Rags to Jazz*, New World 269.

28. Alec Wilder, *American Popular Song: The Great Innovators, 1900–1950* (New York: Oxford University Press, 1972), 36.

29. Lawrence Gushee, liner notes to *Steppin' on the Gas: Rags to Jazz*, New World 269, in *The Recorded Anthology of American Music* (New York: New World Records, 1976), 3. See also Charters and Kunstadt, 33–37.

30. W. C. Handy to James Reese Europe, Jr., February 5, 1947.

31. Europe, "Negro Composer," 64.

32. Charles Hamm calls the last measures of the piece the "first time that music so dominated by percussion had been captured on a phonograph record." See his *Music in the New World* (New York: W. W. Norton, 1983), 402.

33. Gushee, 3.

34. Sissle, 40–45. Arthur Little, Europe's senior officer, has told the story of the 15th Regiment; see *From Harlem to the Rhine: The Story of New York's Colored Volunteers* (New York: Covici and Friede, 1936). There is also useful material in Sissle's "Memoirs of Lieutenant 'Jim' Europe"; Charters and Kunstadt, 63–68; Lewis, 4; Robert Greene, *Black Defenders of America, 1775–1973* (Chicago: Johnson, 1974), 173–74.

35. Europe's biggest problem was finding good reed players. He solved it, interestingly enough, by personally recruiting his entire clarinet section in Puerto Rico.

36. Sissle, 64–65; and Walton, "15th Regiment Band," *New York Age*, 6.

37. Sissle, 65.

38. "Ragtime by U.S. Army Band Gets Everyone 'Over There,'" *St. Louis Post-Dispatch*, June 10, 1918; reprinted in Kimball and Bolcom, 67–68, and in Sissle, 118–20. The French point of view is presented by Gerard Conte in "Jim Europe et les Hellfighters," *Jazz Hot* 243 (October 1968): 8–10. The 369th Infantry "Hellfighters" was the most famous, but by no means the only notable, black band to serve in the war. There were at least six others, the best known of which (Tim Brynn's 350th Infantry "Black Devils," and Will Vodery's 807th) were led by former Europe associates in the Clef Club. Europe, with characteristic modesty, is said to have declared Jack Thomas's 368th Infantry Band the "best in the A.E.F." See, for example, the *New York Age*, February 22, 1919, p. 6.

39. For much of the spring and early summer of 1918, Europe was assigned to his machine gun squadron, and Sargeant Mikell led the band. In that capacity, Europe was the first black officer to lead troops into combat in the war. In June he was gassed and spent several weeks recovering in the hospital.

40. James Reese Europe, "A Negro Explains Jazz," an interview originally published in *Literary Digest*, April 26, 1919, p. 29; reprinted in Eileen Southern, *Readings in Black American Music* (New York: W. W. Norton, 1983), 240.

41. Quoted in Charters and Kunstadt, 68.

42. See Charters and Kunstadt, 70–71.

43. Europe described some of these "jazzing" techniques in "A Negro Explains Jazz," 28, where he also said that he held daily rehearsals of his band "to prevent the musicians from adding to their music more than I wish them to."

44. Quoted in Southern, *The Music of Black Americans*, 354.

45. Schuller, *Early Jazz*, 247.

46. Ibid., 249.

47. See Hamm, *Music in the New World*, 404.

48. Ibid. See also the analysis in Schuller, *Early Jazz*, 249.

49. Gushee, 1.

50. See, among others, Schuller's description in "Europe," 215.

51. Art Napoleon, for instance, claims that the story of jazz in Boston begins with Jim Europe's appearance there after the war. See "Bunker Hill, Baked Beans and Brass," *The Jazz Journal* (February 1968): 4–6.

NEGOTIATING the COLOR LINE: LOUIS ARMSTRONG'S AUTOBIOGRAPHIES

William H. Kenney III

Louis Armstrong, jazz's most influential musician, was also its first and most prolific, black autobiographer. His several autobiographical statements, important titles in an overlooked genre, merit closer attention for what they reveal about the interactions between jazz and ethnicity in the production of popular literature. Armstrong, in both interviews and his own prose, carefully negotiated along America's color line, creating a diplomatic brand of autobiographical performance that balanced his African-American identity against the expectations of editors and the white reading public. Like other major African-American autobiographers before him, Louis Armstrong carefully orchestrated his story, creating edited versions of himself.

Armstrong permitted to circulate three or four different documents that could be called autobiographical statements. The first, which pioneered autobiography by black jazz musicians, was *Swing That Music* (1936), a ghost-written narrative; the second, written by Armstrong himself but edited with a heavy hand, appeared in 1954 as *Satchmo: My Life in New Orleans*; a third, shorter autobiographical interview dominated the April 15, 1966, issue of *Life* magazine and reappeared in a slightly revised form as the book *Louis*

Armstrong—A Self-Portrait. The Interview, edited by Richard Meryman (1966, 1971).

At the time of his first autobiographical statement, Armstrong was recovering from the lowest point of his career; a combination of bad management, the economic depression, and personal difficulties had momentarily arrested his meteoric ascent (Jones and Chilton, 117). In 1932 and again in 1933, Armstrong fled to England and the continent, returning from his second voyage in 1935 when, with the crucial assistance of a new manager—Joe Glaser—he reoriented his career in more commercial directions, becoming a published autobiographer and starring with Fred Astaire and Bing Crosby in the movie *Pennies From Heaven*.

At that time, musical entrepreneurs like John Hammond, publicists, booking agents, and band leaders helped organize and publicize a popular craze for "swing," rhythmic dance band music played by groups of twelve or more instrumentalists combining precise brass- and reed-section work with solo improvisations. The Big Band Swing Era refined folk polyphonies into scored arrangements for disciplined musical technicians, framing the wild, improvisatory spirit with planning and structure. The formula revived and transformed the popular music business, which had been devastated by the economic crisis of 1929–30. Armstrong's first autobiography was heavily influenced by this movement and represented an effort to interpret his life in the light of contemporary developments.

Armstrong had had substantial experience with big bands in Chicago during the 1920s. He had appeared frequently as a solo star with large dance and theater orchestras led by Erskine Tate, Carroll Dickerson, and influential New Yorker Fletcher Henderson. As early as 1929, he had begun to front Luis Russell's twelve-piece band and largely abandoned the small group polyphony featured on his famous Hot Five and Hot Seven recordings for the Okeh Record Company in 1925–27.

Like big band music itself, *Swing That Music* was arranged to communicate comprehensible signals to the general public. The book claims to be Armstrong's account of how New Orleans jazz transcended its raucous, vulgar origins to become a refined art form in the Swing Era. In his book, as in his swing era music, Armstrong was cast in the role of featured soloist in an arrangement written and edited by others. There is little reason to doubt the details of Armstrong's solo on his life story, but a fuller appreciation of

39

what Albert Stone calls the "autobiographical occasion" (1982) requires investigation of his "degree of control over the text" (Stepto, 6). As in his stage performances and work in recording studios, Armstrong played his own solos but delegated authority over a broad range of related activities.

The structure of *Swing That Music* parallels what Robert Stepto has called "eclectic narrative form." At least four different voices speak from its pages, and only one even claims to be Louis Armstrong. *Swing That Music* (vii–x) opens with an "authenticating" introduction by Rudy Vallee, a white bandleader whose own autobiography (1930), like that of Paul Whiteman, antedated Armstrong's. In a twentieth-century musical variant on the nineteenth-century tradition of former slave narratives, Vallee, whose music was well-known to patrons of elite, white watering holes, reassures the reader that Armstrong's life deserves attention. According to Vallee, Armstrong is a "genius," "one of the greatest, if not the very greatest, of all living trumpeters, particularly, of course, in the high register." While granting that his "utterly mad, hoarse, inchoate mumble-jamble" singing might seem to stem from "a chaotic, disorganized mind struggling to express itself," Vallee insists that "those who know anything about modern music recognize his perfect command."

A second narrative voice, that of Horace Gerlach, a British musician/arranger, speaks at the end of this autobiography in a chapter consisting of musicological explanations of Armstrong's jazz, a glossary of his vernacular, and a series of nine transcriptions of solo variations on his original tune "Swing That Music," a well-regarded vehicle for jazz improvisation. Photographs of the nine improvisers —Benny Goodman, Tommy Dorsey, Joe Venuti, Bud Freeman, Red Norvo, Claude Hopkins, Carl Kress, a bass player named Stanley Dennis, and drummer Ray Bauduc—whose names appear on the title page, accompany the transcriptions. Eight of the nine, of course, are white.

In this way, *Swing That Music* offers a sort of conversation between whites that frames the black jazz star's narrative, recreating the structural characteristics of the nineteenth-century former slave narratives that were similarly surrounded by the comments of white abolitionists. Lest anyone miss the editorial appropriation of Armstrong's music, Gerlach concludes that Armstrong's story demonstrates the progress of modern American music from "rigid," "awkward," "unpolished," and "barbaric" "tribal and revival chants" to "refined," "sympathetic," "closely integrated," "softened," and "tempered" strains "flowing with more evenness and suavity" (125).

The autobiographical narrative itself unfolds as a summary of the first thirty-five years of Louis Armstrong's life. In this main section, two voices share the narrative: one may have been Horace Gerlach, and another is a distant echo of Louis Armstrong himself. The former, a formal, grammatically conventional narrator, regularly intrudes upon the story of Armstrong's life to lecture about swing music. This didactic Armstrong voice intervenes whenever an event or dimension in the historical Armstrong's life can be linked to developments in dance band music during the 1930s. As a consequence, the reader's attention is frequently drawn away from Armstrong's personal past and toward an editorial present full of swing.

In one sense, this linking of Armstrong to big band swing reflected the musician's long professional career in New Orleans marching bands and Chicago theater orchestras. He particularly admired swift, accurate sight reading. Despite rumors to the contrary, he had learned to sight read while working for the Streckfus Brothers' Mississippi paddle wheelers from 1921 to 1923 (Randolph interview).

But Armstrong had remained a steadfast proponent of the aural, improvisatory tradition, as well: he fronted, rather than organized, wrote for, or led big bands, using them to set off and frame his instrumental statements of the melody, solo improvisations, and vocals. When he needed composing, arranging, and organizing skills, he hired a musical technician like Horace Gerlach or Zilner Randolph to whom he turned repeatedly in the 1930s. In this sense, then, Armstrong remained more ambivalent about the arranged, planned aspects of swing than either the didactic voice or Gerlach suggested.

The second narrative voice in the main section of *Swing That Music* speaks about actual events in Louis Armstrong's past in a lightly colloquial, vernacular, vaudeville tone. This narrator makes grammatical mistakes, refers to all whites as Mr., Mrs. or Miss, insists that he realizes how very lucky he is to have escaped the seamy poverty of black New Orleans ("Don't you think I don't"), and punctuates reassuring assertions with "Yes, Suh!"

This other Armstrong voice remembers primarily how he moved away from his roots, emphasizing his emigration from New Orleans on the riverboats, Joe "King" Oliver's invitation to come to

Chicago, subsequent moves to New York, and finally his trip to England, where his narrative ends. The cornet virtuoso's early years as a musician are interwoven with a discussion of the all-white Original Dixieland Jazz Band (ODJB) to whom the book is dedicated along with "King" Oliver, Bix Beiderbecke, and guitarist Eddie Lang. The scholarly Armstrong affirms the Original Dixieland Jazz Band's claims to inventing recorded jazz in 1917, with their celebrated Victor Talking Machine Company records, and carefully underlines their visit to England, suggesting thereby that the historical Armstrong had built his career on a white New Orleans musical tradition.

But there are signs of one Armstrong voice dueling with the other for control of this 1936 autobiographical occasion. In the discussion of the Original Dixieland Jazz Band, for example, the didactic voice establishes 1909 as the date at which the group formed, 1913 as the year of their first popularity outside of New Orleans, and 1916 as their big breakthrough at Reinsenweber's Cafe, a popular "lobster place" on Columbus Circle in New York City. This same voice then describes their subsequent triumph in London, something about which an Englishman like Horace Gerlach was likely to be well informed, before the vernacular voice circles back to gently insist that Buddy Bolden, a Negro, "blazed himself into New Orleans with his cornet as early as 1905" (10–15). In addition, the vernacular voice refers to the ODJB as "The Old Dixieland Jazz Band," "The Dixieland Band," and "The Dixieland," stubborn bits of verbal sparring from a black show business professional.

Similarly, the colloquial Armstrong carefully juxtaposes a description of the glamorous nightly migration of the Broadway theater crowd up to Harlem's Cotton Club, Small's Paradise, and Connie's Inn with his own arrival on Broadway from Chicago in a broken-down car, packed with musicians from the Carroll Dickerson band, its radiator spouting jets of steam: "people who had money to spend and time to spend it in came from all over Manhattan to these clubs . . . [but] colored performers had to ride the rods to get there" (89–90).

The four voices in *Swing That Music* speak to various audiences at different times: Vallee, like a master of ceremonies, addresses the general public interested in musical entertainment. The didactic Armstrong voice explains swing for a middle-class audience while the vernacular Armstrong explains his involvement with it. Horace Gerlach concludes by addressing himself mainly to musicians trained in traditional European notation.

The vernacular Armstrong voice is the most interesting of the four and, in the tradition of nineteenth-century Afro-American autobiographies, addresses itself to two kinds of readers—a "fictive reader," a generalist, curious enough about popular music to pick up a book like this one, and an "implied reader" who is more sensitive and more informed than the fictive reader about both jazz and the racial dimensions of American life (Andrews, 29).

The vernacular narrator, for example, manages to manipulate life stories, communicating to the racially aware reader his sense of participating in a stylized autobiographical act calling for tact and diplomacy. The way the vernacular Armstrong described his experiences on a Mississippi paddle wheeler, which he calls the *Dixie Bell* but refers to in subsequent narratives as the *Sydney*, alerts the racially sensitive reader to a form of ethnic performance in which Armstrong manipulates white images and expectations of Negroes.

Armstrong brought the fruits of his long experience in black show business to each of his autobiographical encounters. When summoned to Chicago in 1922 to join Joseph "King" Oliver's Jazz Band, the group was playing for dancing and also backing a vaudeville-style floor show at the Lincoln Gardens. Armstrong subsequently performed at Bill Bottom's Dreamland Cafe, the Sunset Cafe, and the Vendome and Metropolitan theaters, where jazz was thoroughly mixed with stand-up comedy, tap dance, chorus lines of dancing "ponies," vocalists, and skits.

When Armstrong broke into the music business in Chicago, black musical comedy entertainers like "Jazz Lips" Richardson were still "working under cork," following the conventions established by whites in minstrelsy and vaudeville. Jazz was a form of popular entertainment; because several of South Side Chicago's leading clubs were "black-and-tans," cabarets owned by whites who specialized in offering black show business entertainment to interracial audiences, many racial stereotypes survived in early jazz performance. To ensure their own employment and cater to the expectations of much of their public, black jazz entertainers acquiesced in stage sets depicting southern plantations, log cabins, riverboats, levees, and bales of cotton (*Chicago Defender*, October 31, 1925, March 26, 1927).

Like all the other black musicians and entertainers of the

1920s, Armstrong used traditional show business tactics in his performances before the white public. Although he never performed music in blackface, he once appeared in white face, and, in performance, routinely made faces, rolled and popped his eyes, emphasized the size of his mouth by opening it widely in the tradition of black vaudevillian Billy Kersands, spoke in jive, and rushed about the stage, sweating profusely and waving a large white handkerchief.

Economics, as well as minstrel show conventions, encouraged the adoption of these stylized mannerisms. While blacks sometimes managed the clubs, theaters, and dance halls in which Armstrong worked, whites usually owned them. Black managers and performers created the kinds of shows cabaret owners and their customers wanted. *Swing That Music* reproduces the power structures that had dominated Armstrong's relations with the owners and customers of South Side Chicago's black and tans.

This Armstrong autobiography (18–22) employs a double metaphor to suggest the vernacular narrator's attitudes toward his movement away from New Orleans. The darkly threatening image of the cypress swamp where, as a child musician from the Waif's Home, Armstrong retreated to rest from his efforts, under a broiling sun, to entertain a group of picnickers, represents both a refuge sanctified by generations of slave runaways and a confusing point-of-no-return.

Awakening from his nap to pitch blackness, the young Armstrong flees the terrifying, snake-infested swamp and becomes one of the first blacks to play on the Mississippi riverboats. In his second metaphor, he speaks of the Mississippi River as taking the shape of many poorly formed letter M's and W's when viewed on a map, likening his navigation up the river to a young person's lesson in literacy as well as an avenue of assimilation for black New Orleans music, if not its musicians, into the mainstream of white popular music. The vernacular narrator notes his relief in seeing, from the deck, the cypress swamp slide past the northern-bound paddle wheeler, indicating his awareness of the cultural and racial dimensions of his decision to leave New Orleans and perform on the riverboats.

He says little about the personal dimensions of that experience but does relate a story, of which Horace Gerlach could not have been previously aware, about a late night encounter with the ship's captain, "a wonderful old gentleman, with a white beard and bushy eyebrows and under them the keenest eyes" (44–45, 57–58). Anxious about this situation and aware that "all real Mississippi pilots were very proud of being so," Armstrong adroitly flattered his white superior by mentioning *Tom Sawyer* and the fact that Mark Twain had once been a river pilot. The captain registered expected pleasure at Armstrong's complimentary references, eagerly underlining his close personal association with the writer, and promising that, when they should come to it, he would point out to Armstrong "Jackson Island" where Tom Sawyer and his friends had camped. A thousand miles further upstream, again late at night, a sailor abruptly orders Armstrong to the pilot house. Wondering what he might have done wrong, Armstrong follows the mate to the wheelhouse, only to discover that the captain, recalling their earlier conversation, merely wants to point out Jackson Island as promised. In this symbolic incident, the white captain steers the boat with one hand while laying his other "strong," "heavy," "kind" hand on the black man's shoulder; after a lengthy silence during which Armstrong "got a feeling that he had forgotten I was there," the white captain declares that this country is Mark Twain's country. Acutely aware of what was taking place, Armstrong "knew the time had come when I should feel something he wanted me to feel." Nevertheless, the adventures of Tom and Huck seemed remote to Armstrong to whom the island "looked just the same as a hundred other islands we had passed in the river."

This recollection of having gently manipulated and maintained his psychic distance from the all-powerful white captain hints that Louis Armstrong was not the captain of *Swing That Music*. Whether Gerlach, Vallee, or a third party, the book's editor wielded what William Andrews terms "ultimate control over the fate of the manuscript and considerable influence over the immediate future of the narrator" (Andrews, 21). Armstrong, however, remains the captain of his own mind and signals his awareness of these dimensions of the autobiographical process, exercising his memory strategically, monitoring his speech to perform a version of his ethnic identity that seems to correspond to his collaborators' assumptions.

The vernacular narrator speaks softly and may have been heard only by implied readers, but after all the pontificating about musical refinement, art, and swing, he insists that the "smartest" swing men "played the game as it was dished out to them and made their money" in commercial dance bands but kept noncommercial music alive and growing in their after-hours jam sessions (104–9).

Performances of this sort were deeply engrained in Louis Armstrong's personality, and he apparently liked *Swing That Music* enough to write to a correspondent: "Have you seen the 'book that I've written on 'Swing That Music?. It's pretty good and is 'selling like 'Hot Cakes over on this side. . . . If you have'nt seen one let me know and, I will see that you get's one" (Jones and Chilton 142–43). In his voluminous correspondence, Armstrong routinely employed the apostrophe as an opening quotation mark indicating a cliché, a manner of speaking, as in "book that I've written," "Hot Cakes," and "Swing That Music." Editors routinely removed these grammatically incorrect, but significant, stylistic symbols, refining Armstrong's word solos much as swing refined New Orleans jazz.

Armstrong probably had at least a hand in writing *Swing That Music*. From as early as 1922, he wrote a constant stream of letters to friends, fans, and associates of both races, taking evident pleasure in words. His unorthodox and syntactically incorrect writing style vibrates with a humorous irony largely missing from his published works.

> I must say, that I have been 'One Busy' Cat, since I last saw you in dear Ol' Cleveland. . . . I have been rehearsing for my opening at the Cotton Club (where I am now playing). . . . Otherwise I would have written to you a long time ago. . . .
>
> The Show here is real nice. . . . It,s a Variety Show . . . and Packing' 'Em' 'In' 'Nightly. . . . I think the Big show goes in, some time during the middle of next month . . . Which will require some more of those real hard rehearsing days. . . . Ha . . Ha . . . But I am so sure that I can "Take It until I ain't even 'worried. . . . "Tee Hee . . . And if you get a little time drop 'Ol Satch a line or two . . . 'T,would, be most' 'APPRECIATABLE. . . . 'ump,—Did dat come Outa Mee? . . . Ha . . Ha . . . Goodnight and Goodluck to you always.
>
> Am Trumpetblowingly Yours (letter to Kline, October 22, 1939)

This style of writing undoubtedly would have required editing for the general, "fictive" reader, but most of Armstrong's surging energy and pointed ironies were lost in the process. Clearly, he did play the "stage darky," but in a distinctively self-conscious way which, among other things, made clear to the reader that he knew what he was doing. The elipses, apostrophes-cum-quotation marks, and capitalization of clichéd expressions all indicate a distance from the meanings of the words which he typed on the page. The comments on the Cotton Club floorshow take on an ironic twist when expressed in capitalized clichés, followed by references to numbing fatigue, and conclude with minstrel show monologue. Reducing Armstrong's writing to correct prose removed the many signals he had sent to indicate his awareness of playing with minstrel stereotypes.

Telling irony emerges from his use of hyperbole, cliché, and exaggerated exclamations in describing a dance he had played in Atlanta. He commented in a letter to writer Leonard Feather on September 18, 1941:

> We're getting ready to play a swell dance here tonight for the colored folks and the white folks are invited as spectators and I'm tellin you Leonard you never seen such wonderful gatherings in all your life as they do "all down in these parts. . . . Honest they get along down here at these dances just like one'beeg family. . . . It would be 'kicks some times if you could 'Dig some of this jive sos, you can realize just what I am talking about . . . And do these 'Cats Jitterburg? . . . ! Whooooo'Weeeee . . . ha . . . ha. . . .

Armstrong's epistolary style helps clarify his relationship to the vernacular narrator in *Swing That Music*. The differences in prose style between his letters and his autobiography amount to the difference between someone who consciously manipulates images and another who appears to accept them at face value.

Satchmo: My Life in New Orleans, the second Louis Armstrong autobiography, was the first part of a long work that never appeared. Revealingly, he again covered much the same historical ground but framed experiences between his birth and this arrival in Chicago to join Joe "King" Oliver's Orchestra in 1922. Armstrong again emphasized that "good sense and mother-wit, and knowing how to treat and respect the feelings of other people" were central to his success (159).

Although the major events in Armstrong's early life remain the same, *Satchmo* is a more integrated and less didactic narrative. Taking greater control of this autobiographical occasion, Armstrong banished all authenticating introductions and postscripts, producing his own typescript for the first time. According to Dan Morgenstern, director of the Institute of Jazz Studies, *Satchmo's* "words are essentially Armstrong's own, and nothing of importance he did not write has been put in his mouth" (1985).

But Morgenstern has also chosen his words carefully: *Satchmo* reads little, if at all, like Armstrong's letters and sometimes not even like the thermofax typescript titled "Life of Louis Armstrong," a draft of *Satchmo*, which resides in the collections of the Institute of Jazz Studies.[1] In several instances, what an editor at Prentice Hall took to be the "essential" meaning of Armstrong's words, rather than the actual words of the surviving draft, fills the pages of the published autobiography; once again, someone has systematically pruned away the fanciful punctuation, revealing capitalizations, zesty interjections, enthusiastic exclamations, and parenthetical excursions that make Armstrong's letters such a delightful reflection of his personality. As Whitney Balliett (1954) put it a little condescendingly in his review of *Satchmo*: "Perhaps if the publisher had let the manuscript alone—Louis has a written style, typographically and otherwise, that makes E.E. Cummings seem like ladyfingers on a spree—and not hoked it up with grammar and sentences that its author could never have written, this personality might have come closer to the surface."

And not just Armstrong's personality, either. Armstrong's editor changed the entertainer's meaning, as well as his style, and removed many of the author's explicit references to the racial dimensions of his career. For example, in writing about his mother Mayann, Armstrong wrote that she "came from a little town in Louisiana called Butte Louisiana, when they were all but slaves. . . . And her parents, were all Slaves." *Satchmo* omits the phrase, "when they were all but slaves."

So too, *Satchmo*, referring to King Jones, a master of ceremonies in South Side Chicago cabarets during the 1920s, says, "He acted as though he was not a colored fellow, but his real bad English gave him away." Armstrong had actually written: "I dont think Jones was a colored fellow. I think he was from some [West Indian?] Island. He tried to be everything but colored but that real bad english gave him away." The probability that King was not American-born is missing from the edited, published text, which furthermore suggests that all blacks spoke English badly.

As in his music, so in his writing, Armstrong's style was essential to his meaning; it was not what notes or words he chose but how he used them. For example, the following description of white reactions to the black orchestras with which Armstrong played on

the Mississippi paddle wheelers was completely removed from
Satchmo:

> . . . at first, we ran into a lot of ugly moments while we were
> on the band stand. . . . Such as, 'come on 'thar—'black boy,
> etc, . . . We (most of us) were from the South anyway—and
> being used to that kind of jive—we'd—just keep on swinging
> just like 'nothing happened. And before the night was [ob-
> scured] ignored all of that mad jive they'd—layed' on us the
> first part of the evening, and beating out that fine music for
> them in fine fashion - hmmmm, They 'Love us, —'do you hear
> me????—they 'Loved us. . . . We couldn't turn for them sing-
> ing our praises, etc. . . . Telling us to hurry up and come
> back. . . . Cute? . . .

Armstrong's punctuation communicated his sense of irony in unpleasant racial situations over which he had no control. He used
the apostrophe, elipses, and vocal sounds to indicate his perception of another reality behind the dominant white system.

The book called *Satchmo* ends symmetrically with his opening night at the Lincoln Gardens, but the photocopied typescript
called "Life of Louis Armstrong" does not, continuing on for several
pages of recollections about life on Chicago's South Side. One particularly revealing anecdote was removed from *Satchmo*; it would
have communicated to his readers how sensitively attuned black
audiences and musicians were to racial commentary.

Armstrong's story involved the pioneering Original Creole
Band, which had popularized small band ragtime and novelty
music on the vaudeville circuits from 1911 to 1917. According to
Armstrong:

> You looked at Bill and would swear he was a whit[e] boy. He
> had all the features even the voice, yes he really did look like
> an o'fay boy (southern boy) at that. his sense of humor, Oh!
> Boy it was unlimited.

Armstrong proceeds to recall a racially complex routine performed by Johnson and Joe Oliver at the Lincoln Gardens, a cabaret
and dance hall patronized mostly by blacks.

> As opening night progressed every number Joe Oliver's Band
> played was a gassuh. Finally they went into a number called
> 'Excentric', that is the one where Papa Joe took a lot of breaks.
> He would take a four bar break then the Band would play then

he would take four more, at the very last chorus he and Bill
Johnson would do a sort of Act musically, While Joe Oliver
would be talking like a baby, Bill Johnson would pet the baby
in his high voice. That first baby Joe would imitate was suppose[d] to be a white baby. when Joe's horn cried like the white
baby, Bill Johnson would come back with, 'Don't Cry Little
baby.' The last baby was suppose[d] to be a little colored baby,
then they would break it up. Joe would yell, Baaaah! baaaaaaah!
then Bill would shout, 'Shut up you lil so and sooooooooooo.
Then the whole house would thunder with laughs and ap-
plauses. Bill Johnson was really a good Bass man.

Nevertheless, the published version of Armstrong's story does
negate the earlier picture of his steady assimilation into a new
swing mainstream. Published when the Swing Era had run its
course and a post-World War II revival of more traditional jazz styles
was in full cry, *Satchmo* covered only the years between 1900 and
1922, in part to supply information then demanded by traditional
jazz fans.

The Traditional Jazz (or Dixieland) Revival that gripped the
jazz world after World War II embodied a reaction against the com-
mercialization of jazz and the dominance of white bands in the
Swing Era. Leftist writers and jazz fans romanticized the black
working man and the pure folk music he produced in New Orleans.
Some of the best of the earliest American books on jazz emerged
from this school of thought (Ramsey and Smith), and a series of
reissues of early jazz records, most of which swing fans had never
heard, led to "rediscovery" and second careers for such great musicians as Sidney Bechet and Jelly Roll Morton (Collier, *Making of
Jazz*, 281–91).

Not surprisingly, therefore, in *Satchmo* Armstrong confined
himself to his experiences within the black community; he rarely
allowed white characters to distract attention from a detailed description of black New Orleans, filling his story with affectionate
portraits of family, friends, and fellow musicians, making few direct
comments about the surrounding white culture or his relations
with it. In an abbreviated version of his experiences on the Streckfus
Line, Armstrong revealed for the first time that he and the other
black musicians had been strictly segregated but commented
lightly that, because he was from the South, he had "always loved
my white folks" (194–95).

So, too, Armstrong offers strangely hyperbolic comments

about the white cornet star Bix Biederbecke whom he met when the *Sydney* stopped in Davenport, Iowa:

> It was there that I met the almighty Bix Beiderbecke, the great cornet genius. Every musician in the world knew and admired Bix. He made the greatest reputation possible for himself, and we all respected him as though he had been a god. Whenever we saw him our faces shone with joy and happiness, but long periods would pass when we did not see him at all. (209)

Louis manages to praise the white jazzman by juxtaposing hyperbolic images of a godlike white person and all "we" others; he keeps his distance by offering a vaudeville stereotype of "our" greetings to Beiderbecke, slyly shifting the point of view from the welcomers to a third-party observer. At the same time, he indicates that while in Beiderbecke's physical presence, "we" treated him respectfully, but, not "seeing" him for long periods of time, "we" were not obliged to pay him respect.

More important, *Satchmo* recreates a series of vivid pictures of life in black New Orleans, offering in the place of individual introspection, a group biography in which the self is enmeshed in family and neighborhood. In contrast to the orderly, mannered culture of the white middle class, *Satchmo* details the carnivalesque immediacy of life in an ethnic community full of music making and eating and drinking ceremonies. Louis goes to great lengths to affirm his respect for the black community as a whole and those with whom he lived in particular (28). He takes time to describe important cultural rites in the New Orleans ghetto. For example, on his return from his first long, trying voyage on the *Dixie Bell* where, he notes, the hours were long and physically exhausting, he goes out on the town with his mother "to learn how to hold my liquor." In the evening's mounting hilarity, the young musician expresses his strong sense of relief in returning to family and friends ("the people who loved us and spoke our language") from the segregated paddle wheelers (201). Similarly, *Satchmo* ends with the young cornetist's arrival in Chicago where, in addition to joining the Oliver Orchestra, he eagerly participates in ceremonial feasts provided by Stella Oliver. These occasions centered around New Orleans recipes for red beans and rice, thus affirming southern culture in the North. In contrast to *Swing That Music*, therefore, *Satchmo* contains maps of local ethnic ceremonies in which few traces of the dominant white society were allowed to interfere.

But *Satchmo*, like *Swing That Music*, was a performance. The autobiographer refused to speak directly about the arts of impression management in the biracial jazz world; he kept his mask as New Orleans jazzman firmly in place in order to use this autobiographical statement in building a new generation of fans. In private, however, Armstrong was perfectly willing to write about touchy racial matters. In a letter to Betty Jane Holder in 1952 when he was writing *Satchmo*, Louis discussed his reactions to his 1949 appearance at Mardi Gras as King of the Zulus, a symbol of black working-class royalty in New Orleans. The role required that he whiten-up around the eyes and mouth, and wear a long black wig, a crown, red velvet gown, black tights, and a grass skirt (Collier, *Armstrong*, 311–12). Jazz writers and black leaders criticized Louis for "playing the fool" and, contrary to recent commentary, he did entertain serious misgivings about this black man's commentary on the whites' "blacking up." His private account emphasized that he had arrived in the Crescent City after an all-night drive and fell asleep at 6:00 a.m. on parade day morning, only to be awakened by the make-up brush of the Zulu Club representative sent to prepare him for his role as King in that day's parade. He admitted that he and his friends found the make-up "creepy" but reminded his correspondent that his step-father had worn it too; it was, afterall, only make-up for a traditional role in a public performance.

In private correspondence, if not in print, he referred to ugly, hidden, racial dimensions of the beloved Mardi Gras, cherished symbol of the Southern carnival spirit. Armstrong recalled that he had been one of the black men dressed in white robes and carrying large oil lamps who were an important feature of night parades.

> Its lots of people see those guys carrying those lamps, and they,re happy, having lots of fun while during the same. . . . But, let me tell you folks onething. . . . Those 'Cats (meaning) those guys, have to go through an awful set of 'head whippings' in order to get those lamps. . . . And thats just-for that one particular parade. . . . If the parade should start (we,ll say) at—8,o,clock at night,—this gate is opened-at 5-o,clock. Captain Joe is standing there with a big stick that was made from a shovel handle. . . . And—And And—every black sommitch that sticks his head into that gate—saying—,here I am Captain Joe and—as he goes through that gate—Captain Joe whales, him right across his big head with that that stick. . . . Ha ha ha. . . . That Cat'll only smile (of appreciation) as if to say—

Captn Joe-you,s a mess. . . . Very amusing. . . . And thats for
sure. . . . (Armstrong to Feather, June 29, 1953)

In view of hidden horrors like these, his refusal to accept an
invitation from Myra Menville to perform once again in New Orleans is understandable. In a letter dated December 23, 1956, Armstrong replied:

I Sho'd" like to Come back home And blow Some *fine Jive* for
my home folks, But, Since the *AXE* has *hit* All *bands* with 'Ofays
+ 'Spades' together *"MMM"*. Anyway' maybe *later*.

Similarly, in a letter (March 7, 1970) to traditional jazz discographer
Tom Bethell, he noted the racially clichéd press coverage of his
role as a pallbearer in Buddy Petit's 1931 funeral. One Southern
paper reported that as the pallbearers were placing the coffin in
the vault, Armstrong said to Buddy " 'Oh you Dawg.' " Armstrong
insisted that he had said no such thing and suggested that the
reporter was looking for good copy: "New Orleans people 'has always had a wonderful sense of Humor Anyway. Even in Death."

Most important, the limits of Louis Armstrong's control over
this autobiographical occasion were hidden in its title. In a December 21, 1946, letter to *Melody Maker* magazine, a British jazz publication, Armstrong indicated that a British jazz journalist had ren-
dered his then nickname—"Satch"—as "Satchmo" upon meeting
him for the first time. Armstrong wrote that he attributed this slip
to the Englishman's spontaneous reaction to the size of his mouth:
he seemed to have " 'Mo-mouth—so they called me 'Satchmo—
which everybody in America thinks its cute."

The third Armstrong autobiography appeared in two different
versions and again retraced many of the same stories of public
life in black New Orleans that Armstrong had by now reified into
a holy jazz litany—parades, brass bands, funerals, good-hearted
prostitutes, and gangsters—which left many less pleasant things
unsaid. Like the standard New Orleans tunes—"Sleepy Time Down
South," "Dear Old Southland," "Bill Bailey Won't You Please Come
Home" which he played so often—the jazzman trotted-out familiar stories that together formed a special mutual ground, a kind
of jazzy cease-fire zone between blacks and whites. Because neither
of the two versions of this third autobiographical occasion made
any special effort to correct or elaborate upon factual details from
earlier books, they were largely redundant and, in view of the inter-

view format, steps backward toward the era of eclectic narratives over which the subject had only partial control.

The *Life* version carefully sanitized aspects of the Armstrong stories found in the other books; the story of the pistol that sent the youngster to the Waif's Home, for example, became a story of a cap gun. Moreover, *Life* airbrushed the portraits of bordello life, omitted references to religion and violence, and moved incidents about from one to another spot in the narrative.

But in some ways, *Louis Armstrong—The Interview* began to deal with its subject's tactics as an intercultural performer, a subject about which he had spoken only privately before. According to this interview, Armstrong, as far back as 1928, had begun to worry that he would burn himself out as a jazz trumpet player. The jam sessions in after-hours clubs, which followed four shows a day in the theaters and evening appearances in well-known cabarets, lasted well into the morning hours. There was no end to the over-heated world of jazz musicians (7). He felt the need of more career security.

Struggling with serious managerial problems, Louis remembered the tragic fate of his mentor Joe Oliver, a business-oriented band leader who had nevertheless died in poverty, mocked by younger musicians. Armstrong would not allow the same thing to happen to him and began to put "a little showmanship in with the music," to "live for the public." To reach the less musically aware, "fictive" audience, he highlighted plenty of mugging, clowning, and singing of songs made popular in the 1950s and 1960s like *Blueberry Hill*, *Hello, Dolly!*, and *Mack the Knife*. His popularity soared, and he put less pressure on his ravaged lip.

As he admitted, his selection in 1936 of Joe Glaser to be his manager led to his subsequent success as a popular entertainer; the black sheep child of proper, middle-class parents, Glaser had been associated with Southside Chicago's Sunset Cafe, housed in a building his mother owned at 35th and Calumet Streets. In a business dominated by gangsters, Glaser enjoyed sufficient gangland connections to protect his investments. From as early as 1926, he had urged Armstrong to rely more on showmanship than on instrumental virtuosity (Collier, *Armstrong*, 273–78).

Armstrong's description of his own relations with Glaser reiterated the guarded, diplomatic stance toward whites found in *Swing That Music* and *Satchmo*. While he believed that Glaser, a proven ally, genuinely supported his aspirations, Armstrong kept his distance by always addressing him as "Mr. Glaser" (45). The white manager, who felt free to use Armstrong's first name, expressed no awareness of the reasons for Armstrong's avoidance of such intimacy:

> Louis has never failed to take my advice, never failed to respect me, and has been one of the most honorable and faithful guys to me in the world. I guess to me he's like a son. A brother. He's like a younger brother with me. He calls me "Pops." He always called me "Pops." He's never called me "Joe" (*Life*, April 15, 1966).

To help explain Armstrong's relationship to Glaser, Richard Meryman, coauthor of several show business memoirs, included an important paragraph *verbatim* from the typescript of "Life of Louis Armstrong" in his Armstrong "autobiography":

> Those are two things, I learned coming up in New Orleans, and that is (as an old timer told me)—to always have a good white man behind you 'Son, that could put their hands on you (when in trouble) and say—'That's 'My nigger. Which the man proved he was right . . . Anytime we worked for some rich white folks, or white folks—'period . . . We had sort of a feeling that we were more protected than if we had gobs of money . . . It has always been and will always be, in the South,—what white folks you know, and not so much money you have.

Armstrong implied that this southern strategy served him well outside the South.

But Armstrong's appeal to a mass audience required a situational ethnicity in musical performance as well as in autobiographical statements. The popular entertainer of the 1960s, for example, avoided bringing out on stage any unpleasant implications about American racial relations sometimes associated with the lyrics of *Black and Blue* (What did I do . . . ? My only sin is in my skin . . ."). Armstrong insisted that he was on stage to entertain, that serious social problems should be addressed elsewhere.

As in *Swing The Music*, so in this last autobiographical statement, Louis Armstrong communicated an awareness of his role as an ethnic performer, manipulating words and sounds that he judged the public ready to hear. Eventually dubbed "Ambassador Satch" for his constant worldwide touring for the United States Department of State, Armstrong had trained for the role in America, where interracial mediations often required considerable discretion.

The structure of Armstrong's autobiographies closely paralleled that of his musical performances: Armstrong the popular entertainer drew big crowds with his minstrel clowning, willingness to perform popular material readily familiar to the general public as well as feature slapstick vocalists like Velma Middleton, and his own high-note instrumental theatrics; Armstrong the jazz musician included just enough improvisational creativity to remind "implied" jazz fans that he was the man who had made the Hot Five and Hot Seven records. The fictive, musically naive general public would not (and need not) catch the subtleties that the "implied" jazz listener savoured.

The sense of two levels of communication—two messages and two kinds of listeners—was a vital foundation of the jazz concept of "hip." It was hip to identify the fine points of the artistry with which Louis Armstrong performed his shows, to catch the fleeting moments of beauty that he sprinkled through his act. But it was also hip to grasp the racial dimensions of the act and the audience reactions to them. Consciousness of a conflict between surface appearances and underlying reality was hip in both music and autobiography.

In most respects, Armstrong's autobiographical statements paralleled those of the other New Orleans jazzmen of his generation. In chronological order of publication, the stories of drummer Warren "Baby" Dodds, reed star Sidney Bechet, contrabassist George "Pops" Foster, trumpeter Lee Collins, and banjo/guitarist Danny Barker reflect different personalities but describe much the same jazz environment.

Although inspired by Armstrong's books, most other New Orleans jazzmen, Pops Foster excepted, discussed racial dimensions of the jazz world more than "Satchmo." Dodds stressed the fact that racial discrimination forced Negro musicians into entertainment music in the first place (Gara, 3–4). Bechet organized his life story around the murderous white vengeance visited upon his grandfather for courting a white woman (1960). Collins's story works toward a grizzly climax in a state-run mental hospital where the trumpeter was alternately abused and ignored (1974). No other New Orleans autobiographer ever attained Armstrong's fame; their relative obscurity at least permitted them to take more chances. Then, too, the passage of time brought a relatively greater freedom of expression to blacks; Danny Barker's recent autobiography breaks new ground in its sometimes bitter candor about black racial strategies and perceptions (1986).

Louis Armstrong treated autobiography as would a professional performer, playing his role and using his performance to enhance his career. The public Armstrong had less to say about social injustice or personal catastrophe. He emphasized ways to get along, examples of the strategic presentation of the self, and an impenetrable diplomacy; his stories resemble the didactic prescriptions of Benjamin Franklin's autobiography. Like Franklin, Armstrong preached a hard-headed realism, tactical planning, and optimistic activity.

Louis Armstrong's autobiographies will neither directly support nor refute James Lincoln Collier's assertions that Armstrong "was plagued all his life by being unable to put himself forward, stand up to authority, and . . . deal with competition from other males" (*Armstrong*, 30–31). At the same time, no autobiography delivers a fully reliable, realistic portrait, because, as Ralph Ellison notes and this essay demonstrates, each one is "a complex intermixture of public message and personal motive, expressive intention and literary strategy orchestrated by the autobiographer" (*Shadow and Act*, 77–94). Each Armstrong autobiography is equally reliable as evidence of autobiographical occasions and strategies in his life and equally unreliable, *Satchmo* included, as evidence of the "real" Louis Armstrong. But the cool-headed, disciplined, and diplomatic optimism of these stories seems beyond the reach of a broken man longing for applause and approval. As he said casually and in passing to Richard Meryman, "I never let my mouth say nothing my head can't stand."

Note

1. This photocopy of a typewritten document with corrections in Armstrong's hand appears to be an old thermofax duplication. Morgenstern, director of the Institute for Jazz Studies, insists that this document is Armstrong's personal draft of what became *Satchmo*. See Morgenstern's review of *Louis Armstrong: American Genius*, by James Collier. Collier correctly points out, however, that the document could still have been edited before Armstrong corrected it by hand. James Lincoln Collier, letter to the author, August 26, 1988.

References

Andrews, William L. *To Tell a Free Story: The First Century of Afro-American Autobiography*. Urbana: University of Illinois Press, 1986.

Armstrong, Louis. Letter to Tom Bethell. March 7, 1970. Armstrong File. William Ransom Hogan Jazz Archive, Tulane University.

———. Letter to Leonard Feather. September 18, 1941. Armstrong Collection. Institute of Jazz Studies, Rutgers University–Newark.

———. Letter to Leonard Feather. June 29, 1953. Armstrong Collection. Institute of Jazz Studies, Rutgers University–Newark.

———. Letter to Betty Jane Holder. February 9, 1952. (Xerox copy kindly furnished by Douglas Daniels, University of California, Santa Barbara.)

———. Letter to Mr. Kline. October 22, 1939. Armstrong File. William Ransom Hogan Jazz Archive, Tulane University.

———. Letter to *Melody Maker Magazine*. December 21, 1946. Armstrong Collection. Institute of Jazz Studies, Rutgers University–Newark.

———. Letter to Myra Menville. December 23, 1956. Armstrong File. William Ransom Hogan Jazz Archive, Tulane University.

———. "Life of Louis Armstrong." Armstrong Collection. Institute of Jazz Studies, Rutgers-Newark.

———. *Louis Armstrong—A Self Portrait. The Interview*. Edited by Richard Meryman. New York: Eakins Press, 1966, 1971.

———. *Satchmo: My Life in New Orleans*. New York: Prentice-Hall, 1954.

———. *Swing That Music*. London: Longmans, Green, 1936.

Balliett, Whitney. "Good King Louis." *Saturday Review* 37 (November 1954): 54.

Barker, Danny. *A Life in Jazz*. Edited by Alyn Shipton. New York: Oxford University Press, 1986.

Bechet, Sidney. *Treat It Gentle*. New York: Hill & Wang, 1960.

Collier, James Lincoln. *Louis Armstrong: American Genius*. New York: Oxford University Press, 1983.

———. *The Making of Jazz: A Comprehensive History*. Boston: Houghton Mifflin, 1978.

Collins, Lee. *Oh, Didn't He Ramble: The Life Story of Lee Collins as Told to Mary Collins*. Edited by Frank J. Gillis and John W. Miner. Urbana: University of Illinois Press, 1974.

"Corkless Comedy." *Chicago Defender*, October 31, 1925, p. 6.

Ellison, Ralph. *Shadow and Act*. New York: Random House, 1964.

Gara, Larry. *The Baby Dodds Story*. Los Angeles: Contemporary Press, 1954.

Jones, Max, and John Chilton. *Louis: The Louis Armstrong Story, 1900–1971*. Boston: Little, Brown, 1971.

Meryman, Richard. "An Interview with Louis Armstrong." *Life*, April 15, 1966, pp. 92–102, 104, 107–9, 110, 112–16.

Morgenstern, Dan. Review of *Louis Armstrong: American Genius*, by James Lincoln Collier. *Annual Review of Jazz Studies* 3 (1985): 193–98.

———. "Introduction." *Satchmo: My Life in New Orleans,* by Louis Armstrong. New York: DaCapo Press, 1986.

Peyton, Dave. "The Music Bunch." *Chicago Defender,* March 26, 1927, p. 9.

Randolph, Zilner. Interview. Interview File, Institute of Jazz Studies, Rutgers-Newark.

Stepto, Robert. *From Behind the Veil: A Study of Afro-American Narrative.* Urbana: University of Illinois Press, 1979.

Stone, Albert E. *Autobiographical Occasions and Original Acts: Versions of American Identity from Henry Adams to Nate Shaw.* Philadelphia: University of Pennsylvania Press, 1982.

Vallee, Rudy. *My Time is Your Time: The Story of Rudy Vallee.* New York: Oblensky, 1962.

———. *Vagabond Dreams Come True.* New York: Dutton, 1930.

"Vivienne." *Chicago Defender,* October 31, 1925, p. 6.

SOVIET JAZZ: TRANSFORMING AMERICAN MUSIC

Greg Gaut

Jazz, the most influential American music in the twentieth century, has played a major role in the cultural history of the Soviet Union ever since the end of its civil war in the early 1920s. The history of Soviet jazz centers on the epic struggle of Soviet musicians to establish a musical revolution "from below" in the face of the Soviet government's attempts to suppress it "from above." By the late 1960s this battle with the Soviet bureaucracy was largely won. Then, Soviet musicians had created a rich jazz scene with its own history, tradition, stars, and stylistic diversity. No longer an exotic sideshow in the jazz world, they had paid the dues to gain full membership in the international jazz community.

To appreciate their achievement, it helps to understand the obstacles in their path. First, Western influences traditionally generate controversy in Russia. In 1698, for example, Peter the Great shocked and angered his isolated nation by touring Europe and, upon his return, forcing his nobles to cut their beards and wear Western clothes.[1] In the nineteenth century the intellegentsia split into two camps, the Slavophiles and Westernizers, over the issue of Western cultural penetration.[2] In 1937, Josef Stalin exploited Russian xenophobia by charging falsely that his political rivals were

Western spies.[3] Beyond the general fear of the outside, Soviet jazz had to survive the cultural policy of "socialist realism" under which the party demanded that artists replace "bourgeois" forms, including jazz, with new "proletarian" culture.[4] These utopian visions were ultimately abandoned, but even then jazz musicians had to fight a cultural bureaucracy that, if not opposed to jazz as a matter of ideology, mistrusted anything independently organized and spontaneously created. On another front, jazz musicians had to defend themselves against the familiar puritans and high-culture philistines who attack or ignore jazz everywhere. Throughout they were isolated by geography, politics, race, and culture from the creative center of the music.

To create a thriving jazz scene in these conditions was an accomplishment, but mere emulation of someone else's music, however successful, was not enough. For more than two decades, the most innovative Soviet musicians have aimed for nothing less than transforming this American music into something distinctively their own. Divergent approaches have emerged, including the avant garde movement represented by the Ganelin Trio and the merger of jazz and Soviet folk music examplified in the work of Azerbaijani pianist Vagif Mustafa-Zadeh. Musicians and jazz enthusiasts everywhere can be enriched by Soviet attempts to experiment with the music after they have mastered it.

Only in the 1980s did the world of Soviet jazz become visible to the American jazz audience.[5] Soviet jazz records became available, and Soviet musicians began touring in the United States. The new presence of Soviet jazz has helped dismantle long-standing Cold War stereotypes. Americans are taught that the Soviet Union, or "Russia" as we still like to call it, is a "totalitarian" society where impotent, atomized people are totally controlled by the KGB. The fact that Soviet musicians successfully created a jazz tradition enriches our knowledge of Soviet society by forcing a revision of the conventional wisdom.[6]

Riding the Whirlwind: The History of Soviet Jazz

Soviet jazz musicians built the sophisticated scene they have today with an inspiring tenacity and a deep devotion to the music. Their remarkable history is reconstructed in S. Frederick Starr's excellent book, *Red and Hot: The Fate of Jazz in the Soviet Union*.[7] Both a historian and a jazz musician, Starr respectfully chronicles the history of Soviet jazz, beginning in 1922 when Valentin Parnakh, a Russian futurist poet, heard New Orleans jazz in Paris and came home to organize the first Soviet jazz band. This band enlivened two productions of the avant garde theatre director Vsevolod Meierhold.[8] In 1926 jazz began in earnest, following the tour of several U.S. bands, including Benny Peyton's Jazz Kings which featured Sidney Bechet on clarinet.[9] In the open cultural atmosphere of the New Economic Policy (NEP) between 1921 and 1929, jazz found an enthusiastic audience, at least among the educated urban elite.

But the ascendancy of Stalin in 1928 led to a clampdown. Throughout the cultural sphere, the hands-off cultural policy of the NEP was suddenly replaced by vigorous state intervention and control. Artists of all kinds were forced to join professional organizations that monitored access to the public and determined appropriate style and content. The Association of Proletarian Musicians became the censorship body for music, and it quickly turned against jazz.[10] The key document was novelist Maxim Gorky's "On the Music of the Gross," published in *Pravda* on April 18, 1928.[11] He argued that jazz was linked to unrestrained sexuality, which in turn was a symptom of the decline of decadent bourgeois civilization. He acknowledged that it was rooted in the oppression of American Negroes but claimed that they had abandoned jazz after it was discovered by middle-class whites.

For several years the party harrassed jazz musicians, but it had an insoluble problem: it really wanted to create a totally new culture for the Soviet masses. By 1932 when no new culture had emerged, jazz began to fill the vacuum, leading to a brief but vibrant "red jazz age." There were new "dzhaz" bands everywhere, and even a few jazz "stars" like Alexander "Bob" Tsfasman, the leader of the first Soviet big band that could really swing, and Leonid Utyosov, the popular band leader who starred in the 1934 film *Happy Guys*, which climaxes with a riotous scene in which his big band takes over the Bolshoi Theatre in a symbolic overthrow of high culture by the sensual, spontaneous popular culture of jazz.[12]

But the days of the happy guys were cut short by the Stalin purges that began in 1936. A few musicians were personally swept up in the purges, while jazz itself was put on the defensive by renewed attempts to make music fulfill a propaganda function. Jazz never disappeared, but it was forced to assume a low profile. Hitler's invasion of the Soviet Union changed everything. Jazz was "rehabilitated" to aid in the war effort. Jazz bands with names like the Red Flag Baltic Fleet Jazz Orchestra entertained heroically at the front, and many jazz players paid with their lives.[13] Tsfasman and Utyosov were active, and Eddie Rosner, a displaced Polish Jew who idolized Harry James, emerged as the new star of Soviet jazz. His State Jazz Orchestra of Byelorussia played one thousand concerts in forty cities during the war. Frederick Starr believes that the powerful, full-blooded sound of Rosner's band was the high point of Soviet swing.[14]

The xenophobic backlash following the end of World War II was especially hard on jazz musicians, champions as they were of music imported from the West. This was the low point of Soviet jazz. Rosner was sent to Siberia, saxophones were confiscated, and bands that survived had to change their repertoires and their names, dropping the word "dzhaz" for something innocuous like "variety music." But jazz survived even through this period. Eddie Rosner managed to form a jazz band in the Gulag.[15] Oleg Lundstrem's big band was exiled from Moscow to a tiny provincial town, but he soon managed to negotiate gigs in the provincial capital of Kazan, where his band was soon playing their Ellington charts with exuberance and courage.[16] The Baltic republics—the independent states of Estonia, Latvia, and Lithuania that the Soviet Union occupied prior to the war and never gave back—became the relatively free zone of Soviet culture during this period. Cultural control was pushed to its limit and found wanting, unable to either destroy the resilience of the musicians or replace jazz with an alternative culture that was really popular.

In the early 1950s some young Soviets found in the bebop style an ideal expression of their alienation. The small alienated subculture known as the "stiliagi" (style hunters) wore zoot suits and long hair and sought an "authentic" personal life as an alternative to the public life they found empty.[17] Jazz musicians and fans operated as a kind of semideviant cult. Fueled by the Voice of America jazz broadcasts, hundreds of combos sprang up. By the time de-Stalinization and the "thaw" allowed a few European jazz bands to visit, Soviet jazz musicians had created their own bebop scene, making up for the time lost in the postwar reaction. Meanwhile, a big band revival was sparked by Oleg Lundstrem's return to Moscow in 1957 and Benny Goodman's successful tour of the Soviet

Union in 1962, the first tour by an American jazz band since 1926. Khrushchev attended his Moscow concert, but the highpoint was the all-night jam sessions in Leningrad and Moscow hotels where band members Zoot Sims, Mel Lewis, and others jammed with some of the best Soviet players.[18]

In Starr's opinion, Soviet jazz reached its apogee in 1965–1967, but the new jazz of the Soviet 1960s developed more as an art music for the cognoscenti than as the popular dance music it had once been.[19] Its favored venue was the festival, and the Tallinn, Estonia, festival became the highlight of the Soviet jazz year beginning in 1957. The first Moscow festival was in 1962, and soon festivals were organized in other cities. The 1967 Tallinn Festival featured twenty-eight Soviet bands, several European bands, and the American Jazz Quartet led by Charles Lloyd and featuring Keith Jarrett, Ron McClure, and Jack DeJohnette.[20] Starting in 1962, a few Soviet jazz musicians were able to travel to the Warsaw and Prague festivals, and later they were able to travel to Western Europe.

In the 1960s Melodiya, the state record monopoly, issued its first jazz records, jazz began to be heard on the radio, and jazz societies sprung up even in small towns. Jazz criticism reached a sophisticated level, as exemplified by the work of Alexey Batashev, whose book on the history, development, and contemporary directions of Soviet jazz was published in 1972.[21] The party had decided to accommodate itself to jazz, moving from a strategy of suppression to one of regulation and cooptation.

The new official attitude toward jazz was indicated by the "Jazz" entry in the third edition (1972) of the authoritative and rigorously ideological *Great Soviet Encyclopedia*. Written by jazz educator Leonid Pereversev, it gives a brief history of Soviet jazz, acknowledging the contributions of Parnakh, Tsfasman, Utyosov, Rosner, and others. Instead of branding jazz as a sympton of bourgeois decadence, jazz is now defined as a "genre of professional musical art." Pereverzev concludes with a Marxist analysis that might find U.S. supporters: "Contemporary or modern jazz is developing through a struggle between two different tendencies: so-called commercial jazz, which is an integral part of the bourgeois entertainment industry, and creative jazz, which is seeking new artistic methods."[22]

Another sign of changing attitudes was the Soviet film *Jazzman*, an entertaining musical comedy that actually satirized the Stalinist cultural policies of the 1930s.[23] The film opens with

Kostya, an earnest young piano student at an Odessa conservatory, standing "trial" for playing jazz. The year is 1928, and the Stalinist cultural revolution is just beginning. He is charged with popularizing bourgeois decadence and becoming a tool of imperialism. Not so, argues Kostya, jazz is the revolutionary music of the Negroes, the oppressed people of the United States. Kostya is expelled, but he finds three down-and-out street musicians and sets out on a picaresque journey to establish his new jazz band in this hostile environment. In the closing scene, a flashforward to the 1960s, the aged musicians are playing in a huge concert hall, having triumphed over the Stalinist cultural policy.

There is one flawed moment in this otherwise savvy film. The "famous jazz singer," clearly suggestive of Billie Holiday, who visits Moscow is said to be from Cuba. The director, concerned perhaps about the Cold War xenophobia of the censors, took the safe road of portraying the foreigner as a Soviet ally rather than adversary. This false note is compounded by the portrayal of the black jazz singer by Soviet actor Larissa Dolina.[24] Her scenes seem awkward to American eyes, but perhaps not to Soviet audiences, isolated as they are from Afro-American culture. Otherwise, this solid jazz film openly ridiculed the Stalinist notion that popular culture can be imposed "from above."

As it turned out, not state suppression, but the invasion of rock and roll, undercut jazz in the late 1960s.[25] Just as elsewhere in Europe, it quickly won the allegiance of the young and took the place of jazz as the music of sensuality and dance. It also captured the attention of those party bureaucrats and academics who are concerned about what they see as the declining values of Soviet youth and who regularly write alarmist pieces in the press. Indeed, rock's hold on the imaginations of Soviet youth continues and seems stronger than ever, represented by a core of officially supported professional bands and untold hundreds of unofficial, semi-underground bands in every city.[26]

Soviet Jazz Today: The Age of Maturity

The rock deluge undercut the popularity of jazz, especially with Soviet youth. Like its counterparts around the world, Soviet jazz had to react to the new situation as best it could. The period of adjustment is over, and the scene that has emerged has a broad stylistic range, including traditional, mainstream, big band, fusion and free/avant garde jazz, in other words, the same spectrum of styles popular in the United States or Western Europe.

Avant garde jazz, which I discuss below, is particularly vital in the Soviet Union, but the majority of musicians play mainstream jazz. Among the few Soviet mainstream players who can be heard on records available in the United States are Alexei Kuznetsov, the best-known Soviet jazz guitarist, Vagif Mustafa-Zadeh, the world-class pianist from Soviet Azerbaijan who died in 1979 just as he was reaching international fame, and Igor Brill, a pianist who like many Soviet musicians seems to specialize in eclecticism and could just as easily be classified as a fusionist.[27] This is just the tip of the iceberg.[28]

Fusion is also firmly established in Soviet jazz, as represented by Arsenel, organized in 1977 by Moscow saxophonist Alexei Kozlov, who moved from "cool" jazz in the late 1950s to hard bop in the 1960s and finally concluded that fusion was more democratic than other forms of jazz. Arsenel is a sophisticated outfit in the 1970s tradition of the Mahavishnu Orchestra and Weather Report.[29]

Finally, there is traditional and big band jazz. The elder statesman of the Soviet big band scene, and probably of the world big band scene, is Oleg Lundstrem, whose band has performed continuously under his leadership since 1934. For decades this band was a creative force worthy of the Ellington material it specialized in and a haven for some of the best Soviet soloists.[30] Soviet musicians have also been busy reviving and preserving traditional jazz since the 1950s, as evidenced by the Leningrad Dixieland Jazz Band and a host of others.[31]

Even before Mikhail Gorbachev came to power, Soviet jazz enjoyed a measure of state support. Undoubtedly, the party's desire to control and coopt jazz was the essential motivation behind this support, but it nevertheless encouraged the development of jazz. Established annual jazz festivals were supported (e.g., Autumn Rhythms in Leningrad, Summer Rhythms in Riga, and Moscow Jazz Festival, etc.) and new festivals were organized (e.g., Tbilisi Festival in Georgia, Siberian Jazz Days in Novosibirsk, etc.) One Soviet critic estimated that there were 150 festivals between 1967 and 1985.[32] The state also sponsored jazz education. Jazz academies began to be established in the early 1970s at the urging of big band leader and composer Yuri Saulsky. These schools give young jazz musicians the academic training necessary for easy access into professional music jobs. At the 1984 Moscow festival, a special concert of student bands was dedicated to the tenth anniversary of the introduction of jazz education, and some festivals are even devoted to student jazz.[33]

However, Soviet jazz musicians had many complaints about their professional status and their limited access to audiences, all flowing from their position within a system in which all cultural activity was officially controlled by the state. In general, membership in the musicians' organization was prerequisite for playing in a concert or at other official venues; nonprofessional musicians still found audiences, but only by finding sympathetic cracks in the system. Until the last few years, only a small handful of Soviet jazz musicians, and not necessarily the best ones, were "professionals."[34] Access to audiences plagued even these musicians. Although the festival circuit in the Soviet Union is extensive, it has been almost the only place to hear jazz; nightclubs, as we know them, do not exist. There has been no 52nd Street in Leningrad or Moscow.

Freedom to travel, even within the Soviet Union, was also bureaucratically controlled. This made it difficult for Soviet musicians from different citites to interact with each other, much less with Western musicians. In addition, until the Reagan-Gorbachev summits, the level of cultural exchanges between the United States and the Soviet Union was low. Few American musicians of any kind played in the Soviet Union, deepening Soviet isolation from the international scene and especially from the creative center of U.S. music. This isolation significantly limits Soviet jazz. "Jazz has become a world music," German critic Joachim Berendt has written, but "the path-breaking and style-setting musicians still come from America."[35]

The new *glasnost* (openness) policies of Mikhail Gorbachev have had an enormous impact on cultural life in the Soviet Union. Perhaps the most profound change has come in the film industry, where Elem Klimov, an internationally respected director whose films had sometimes run into trouble with the censors, was elected head of the Soviet Filmmakers Union and began to loosen restraints on directors.[36] Important films that had been held up by censors, such as Tengiz Abuladze's anti-Stalinist *Repentance*, were then released. Meanwhile stormy meetings in the Writers Union led to the first Soviet publications of long suppressed works by dissident writers, including Boris Pasternak's *Doctor Zhivago*, and even provocative works by foreign authors such as George Orwell's *1984* and *Animal Farm*.[37]

Jazz too has felt the freshening winds of *glasnost*. Tours by musicians, in both directions, have increased. There was much room for improvement on the Soviet side. The tours by the Ganelin Trio in 1986 and Leningrad Dixieland Jazz Band in 1987 marked the first performance by real Soviet jazz musicians, not counting emigrés, in the United States. In the last several years, the ROVA Saxophone Quartet, Pat Metheny, Dave Brubeck, and Billy Taylor have played in the Soviet Union. Moscow jazz critic Alexey Batashev reported that one Brubeck concert was filmed for Soviet television and another released by Melodiya as a "Live in Moscow" album.[38]

A few new jazz clubs have opened, including the Bluebird in Moscow and the Seaman's Club in Leningrad.[39] The new government policy to allow small-scale private enterprise may lead to increasing numbers of small clubs presenting jazz and greater freedom in managing these clubs. Some Soviet musicians are trying to push these new freedoms farther. Stas Namin, leader of the hugely popoular Moscow rock group that bears his name, has established the "Moscow Musical Youth Center" in Gorky Park. According to news reports, Namin has apparently created the first center for independent production of rock music and videos.[40] If this trend continues, Melodiya's total monopoly over production and distribution of records might end. Since the state record company has released only 250 jazz titles in thirty years and the catalog is limited to the jazz of "professional" musicians, Soviet jazz could benefit greatly from *glasnost* in the area of production and distribution of records.

These developments are encouraging, but it should not be forgotten that Soviet musicians built a deep and vital scene primarily during the Brezhnev era. The continuing vitality of jazz in the Soviet Union can best be judged by recent festivals, which demonstrate that jazz has spread thoughout the Soviet Union's wide expanse and that young musicians are joining the aging generation of the 1950s and 1960s who established the current scene. The 1986 Tbilisi festival in Soviet Georgia, for example, featured forty-four groups and twenty-two soloists from ten of the Soviet Union's fifteen republics, and the music from the non-Russian Soviet cities like Baku (Azerbaijan), Tashkent (Uzbekistan), and Alma Ata (Kazakhstan) made a particular impression.[41] Recently, festivals were held in Cheboksary on the Volga, Novosibirsk in Siberia, and even in Khabarovsk in the Soviet Far East. Given the sophistication of Soviet jazz and its ability to attract new adherents from all over the culturally diverse Soviet Union, it is likely that the music will have an internal dynamism for the foreseeable future.

Toward a New Soviet School of Jazz?

It is no surprise that the various peoples of the Soviet Union, who have long and rich cultural histories of their own, would not be satisfied with the mere competent reproduction of jazz music. According to Soviet jazz critic Alexander Medvedev, when Soviet musicians listened to the best American and European jazz in the 1960s they realized they had much to learn, but "the experience of past years showed that imitation would lead to nothing; they would have to learn to create their own jazz."[42] Responding to the challenge of building a uniquely Soviet school of jazz, Soviet musicians have moved in two different directions: the avant garde or "new jazz" of musicians like Vyacheslav Ganelin and Sergey Kuryokhin on the one hand, and the jazz/folk music blend so prevalent in the Soviet Caucasus and Central Asia. Both have produced interesting musicians and impressive results, but the question of a new school remains open.

The Avant Garde

The one Soviet jazz group of the 1980s that most jazz enthusiasts are likely to recognize is the Ganelin Trio, the most prolific and respected Soviet jazz group of the decade, recognized not only in the Soviet Union but also throughout Europe.[43] Their cause was championed in the West by Soviet emigré Leo Feigin, whose Leo Records has issued a wide selection of their music.

Leo Records has also given significant exposure to other musicians of the avant garde, beginning with two solo records by pianist Sergey Kuryokhin, a talented and complex Leningrader who acknowledges no artistic boundaries in his music. His other Leo albums feature a duo with Boris Grebenshchikov, a collaboration with gypsy vocalist Valentina Ponomoreva and young sax phenomenon Igor Butman, and an appearance with free saxophonist Anatoly Vapirov. He can also be heard playing keyboards for Boris

69

Grebenshchikov's rock group Aquarium on the album *Red Wave: Four Underground Bands from Leningrad,* and he leads the outrageous music/theatre orchestra Popular Mechanics, which was filmed by the BBC for the television series "Comrades," shown by PBS in the United States.[44]

Two other avant garde combos featured by Leo Records come from unlikely places. Homer Liber, the free jazz group most clearly influenced by black American free jazz, especially Coltrane, Ayler, and Coleman, comes from Novosibirsk, Siberia.[45] Critics see a Sun Ra influence in Arkhangelsk, a sextet from the White Sea city of the same name. Alexey Batashev wrote that they were a highlight of the 1984 Moscow Festival; their Leo Records album is a bootleg of a Leningrad concert from the same year.[46]

The 1986 tour of the Ganelin Trio demonstrated the achievements of Soviet jazz and perhaps also the effects of its isolation. The trio first attracted European attention at the Warsaw Jazz Jamboree in 1976 and established their reputation in Western Europe during an extensive tour of England and Wales in 1984.[47] By 1986, the three were playing together only on international tours, and Ganelin and Tarasov were joined by Petras Vishnyauskas at the 1986 Tbilisi Festival, even though Chekasin was also on the program. In 1987, Ganelin emigrated to Israel. Even before that, Vladimir Chekasin has been involved in separate projects, three of which are featured on Leo albums, including an experimental big band album, while Ganelin and Tarasov had released a duo album and Tarasov a solo album on Melodiya.[48]

The group preferred the title Ganelin-Tarasov-Chekasin, and indeed the trio was a kind of supergroup composed of musicians each of whom is an institution in his own right. Pianist Vyacheslav Ganelin, master of piano, synthesizer, and basset, was born to a Jewish family near Moscow in 1944, but his family moved to Vilnius, Lithuania, when he was a boy. After graduating from the conservatory, he became music director of the Russian Drama Theatre there. Percussionist Vladimir Tarasov grew up in Arkhangelsk but moved to Vilnius after a fateful jam session with Ganelin. He also plays with the Lithuanian State Symphony Orchestra.[49] While touring in Siberia, Ganelin and Tarasov met Vladimir Chekasin, who already had a reputation as a driving, innovative, and unpredictable sax player. He, too, moved to Vilnius, where he teaches at the conservatory.

After hours at their regular jobs, they developed a unique approach, a kind of "free jazz" they call "polystylistic." They continually integrated sounds ranging from Dixieland to native folk to chamber music into their sound. Each composition, a kind of "suite" building on a unified idea, lasted about forty minutes. The publicity for their U.S. tour compared them to the Art Ensemble of Chicago, but their music was not based on the blues, funk, or African music; indeed, their relationship to jazz itself was controversial. It may be more accurate to say that it was grounded in those uniquely Russian "blues," that vision of life as grotesque (see the stories of Nikolai Gogol) and transcendental (see Fyodor Dostoevsky's novels), or in the Russian avant garde of the early twentieth century, especially the futuristic poems of Vladimir Mayakovsky and Velimir Khlebnikov.[50]

The comparison to the Art Ensemble was apt to the extent that these musicians too are fluent on many instruments and gave bluntly theatrical performances. In performance, each musician was a self-contained show, but the trio itself sounded as tight as their fifteen years together would suggest.[51] Ganelin sat quietly behind his grand piano piled with basset and synthesizers, passively watching his colleagues while pouring out harmony and bass line. Tarasov handled all manner of percussion in a businesslike fashion behind his drum set, but he might suddenly jump up and attack the piano strings with two small cymbals. Chekasin played various clarinets and saxophones in a coarsely expressive style, sometimes keeping time by stomping on the stage. At the climax of the piece, he became a whole sax section, blowing two saxes fingered independently, one in each hand. Their overall effect was simultaneously heady, passionate, and humorous. Much of their appeal was related to the fact that they were serious musicians who did not take themselves too seriously.

Perhaps the critical controversy they provoked during their U.S. tour testified to their stature as artists.[52] Overall their Town Hall appearance at the JVC Jazz Festival in July 1986 was coolly received by the New York critics. Peter Keepnews of the *New York Post* concluded that they just did not swing, and "for all that fevered activity, the Ganelin Trio's music came across as stiff and indulgent." This was more charitable than Patricia O'Haire in the *Daily News* who remarked that the "Chinese water torture is a jolly game compared to what the Russians just sent to us."[53] Gary Giddins was disappointed by the concert, finding it too familiar: "Euro-free jazz, the mixture as before."[54] Jon Pareles felt that the "trio's extraordinary musicians know how to make abstract music swing," but his brief review was unenthusiastic.[55] East Wind producer Steve Boulay reported that one hundred people walked out of their concert.[56] He continued, however, that they were received enthusiastically when they played with the ROVA Saxophone Quartet in San Francisco.

The lukewarm American reviews were in sharp contrast to the articles collected by Leo Feigen in *Russian Jazz: New Identity*, which purports to take up the story of Russian jazz where Frederick Starr's *Red and Hot* ends, but is more like a polemic in support of the avant garde. According to Feigen, the jazz that Starr wrote about was "entertainment" music to which nothing new was added by Russian musicians. But the emergence of the avant garde changed everything. "The new aesthetic helped Soviet jazz make a crucial step from being a light entertainment music to becoming a serious art form. New music helped the Soviet musicians to find their identity. They stopped aping Americans. They rediscovered the links with the traditions of great Russian culture, corroded by the October Revolution in 1917."[57] For Feigen and his collaborators, this new aesthetic was exemplified in the music of the Ganelin Trio and the other avant garde musicians, on whose behalf extravagant claims were made. Efim Barban, an emigré Soviet jazz critic, wrote that the new Russian jazz "is capable of breathing new life into Western jazz" because it is "perhaps the most dynamic and life-enhancing artistic manifestation of the jazz process in the world today."[58] Another article argued that "they represent the only possible alternative as a retort to the reified, alienating pseudo-art which has become a simple merchandise to bring material profit."[59] Sergei Kuryokin went even further, arguing that jazz of "free" groups like the Art Ensemble or Sun Ra is aesthetically dead and must be replaced by "serious" avant garde music. He rejected the "world music" tendency of jazz, suggesting "that this 'universalization' is a negative process which destroys the distinctive features of personality, and will lead to a degeneration of culture."[60]

Essentially, the Ganelin Trio's supporters sought to position them at the forefront of the international avant garde, and perhaps they made a good case. The music of the Ganelin Trio was both mesmerizing and challenging, but something was missing. The power of jazz lies in the confrontation of Afro-American and European music, and as Joachim Berendt wrote, "it loses its fundamental rationale when one or the other element is overemphasized."[61] Their relative isolation forced musicians like the Ganelin Trio to create their own jazz, but their music suggests at least three ways in which they might benefit from contact with the international jazz community.

First, their music is not just abstract, but often cerebral. Jazz, according to Ornette Coleman, should speak both to the mind and the body. Soviet jazz could stand a shot of funk in the form of the "free funk" (or "no wave" or "funk jazz" or whatever) of American musicians like Ornette Coleman, Ronald Shannon Jackson, James "Blood" Ulmer, who think that jazz should engage not only the mind but be "body music" as well.[62] Indeed, "funk jazz," or for that matter, funk, blues, or soul-based popular music, seems strangely absent from the Soviet jazz, rock, and pop scenes, even though the music is otherwise sophisticated and diverse.

Second, to the extent that the avant garde has become narrowly focused on the messianic nature of its own "Russianness," it might benefit from contact with "world music" influences on jazz and the healthy notion that the interplay of styles from both North and South America, Africa, Asia, and Europe can only strengthen the music. Musicians in Moscow and Leningrad can find "world music" without leaving the USSR, but Russians like Leo Feigen seem to forget the cultural diversity of the Soviet Union. Feigen titled his book *Russian Jazz* and objects to the term "Soviet," which he says refers to the political system and official culture. The word, "Russian," in his view, refers "to the people on whom this Soviet system was imposed—to unofficial culture."[63] However, only 52 percent of Soviet citizens were Russian in 1979, down from 54.6 percent in 1959. It is estimated that by 2000, more than 20 percent of the Soviet population will be from a Muslim ethnic group.[64] Substituting "Russian" for "Soviet" overlooks almost half of the population and sounds like the Russian chauvinism of Tsarist days. Ironically, Vyacheslav Ganelin, the key figure in revival of Russian culture envisioned by Feigen, was by nationality not a Russian but a Jew who lived most of his life in Lithuania until his emigration to Israel.

Finally, Soviet jazz of all styles seems to have lost the political implication it had in the 1950s when it was a key symbol of opposition to the status quo. Now, jazz is attractive purely as music rather than as a "comprehensive metaphor of a free life."[65] Soviet commentators acknowledge that for some American musicians, jazz is a form of social protest, but there is a tendency to maintain that the situation in the USSR is "totally different."[66] To a certain extent, depoliticization is the price of success, the result of moving from the underground to the concert halls. And the Soviet Union is clearly not the totalitarian state of American stereotypes. Still Soviet musicians might profitably consider the example of Miles Davis, Abdullah Ibrahim, Charlie Haden, the Art Ensemble of Chicago, and others who give their music an artistic edge by remaining conscious of political realities and by taking a stand against oppression in their homelands and abroad.

Frederick Starr himself contributed an article to Feigen's *Russian Jazz*, in which he argues that Soviet jazz history has passed through the swing and bop phases and is now in its "free jazz" phase, characterized by the "movement" led by Ganelin. His statement that it is obvious "that the locus of innovation in Soviet jazz has shifted to this movement" may surprise readers of his *Red and Hot*, which barely mentions free jazz. In his view, this movement might be only a passing fancy, unless "it creates a new place for jazz within Soviet culture as a whole."[67] He is suggesting, I think, that Soviet free jazz in its most uncompromising form has the possibility of redefining the relationship between the avant garde and society. But this fascinating possibility should be treated skeptically.

Brewing World Music at Home

Before the emergence of the avant garde, Soviet musicians and critics generally looked to the fusion of jazz and folk music as the most likely answer to the question of how to develop a Soviet jazz style. In his 1972 book, critic Alexey Batashev wrote that the "jazz and folklore" issue had captured the attention of all the main tendencies of Soviet jazz and that "it was exactly by going down this road that the most artistic results, marked by authentic innovation, are being achieved."[68] Surveying some leading composers and musicians of the time, he concluded that the problem was difficult but solvable. In a sequel to Batashev's book published fifteen years later, Alexander Medvedev still felt that "the interaction of folklore and jazz was the key problem of contemporary jazz music." He was disappointed, however, that what had been accomplished in the interim was "only a modest beginning."[69]

Batashev wrote that the difficulty was to produce a synthesis with folk music which lent itself to quality improvization. This was where experiments often ran aground, as jazz composer Yuri Saulsky explained: "The basic theme of the song was stated more or less successfully in a Russian character but in improvisation, which articulated all the themes in blues notes, neither the mood, nor the scale, nor the character of the theme's intonation was maintained. It was as if the theme and improvization 'conversed' in diverse musical 'dialects.'"[70] Already in the early 1970s there was reason to believe that the folk music of the republics of the Soviet Caucasus (e.g., Azerbaijan, Armenia, Georgia) and Central Asia (e.g., Uzbekistan, Kazakhstan) would provide a more fruitful basis than the Slavic (Russian, Ukrainian, Byelorussian) folk musics. Not surprisingly, several Soviet musicians interviewed by Batashev were very interested in John Coltrane's experimentation with African and Asian folk music. Musician/composer Georgii Garanian argued that listeners had become alienated from the abstraction of jazz and stated his preference for the later records of Coltrane over the Miles Davis of "Nefertiti": "because there are strong emotions in this music, clear dramatics, and much precedes from folk scales close to our audio perception. The connection with folk culture is not formalistic, but is in fact a deeply-felt one, poured out in the musician's hot persuasiveness, and this makes his creation a success."[71]

As it turned out, the main growth areas of Soviet jazz in the 1980s were in the non-Russian areas of the country. That there would be a thriving jazz scene in the Baltic republics like Estonia is no surprise because they have been a jazz center for decades.[72] But a "national" stream of Soviet jazz emerged in the capitols of the republics of the Soviet south, including groups from Baku (Azerbaijan), Yerevan (Armenia), Tashkent (Usbekistan), and Alma Ata (Kazakhstan). Little of this music has been heard in the West, but it appears that a conscious attempt to fuse jazz with ethnic music underlies the approach of many of these groups.

This trend was pioneered by Vagif Mustafa-Zadeh, a world-class pianist from Baku, the Soviet oil port on the Caspian Sea whose cultural heritage is Turkish and Islamic.[73] Beginning in the early 1960s he studied Oscar Peterson, Bill Evans, and Thelonius Monk and developed into perhaps the best technical jazz pianist in the Soviet Union. He released six albums on Melodiya and starred at jazz festivals at Tallinn and Tblisi. Just before his death in 1979 (he was only thirty-nine), he won the first prize for composition at the Monaco international jazz festival, attracting European attention for the first time. In his last years, he was moving beyond the mere quotation of Azerbaijani folk melodies and harmonies, experi-

75

Greg Gaut

menting with the total integration of "moogam," the Azerbaijani folk style, into his jazz music.

Fortunately, East Wind Records issued a Mustafa-Zadeh album in the United States, a repressing of a 1979 Melodiya release that caught him in transition between mainstream and ethnic experimentations. Fronting a trio composed of Tamaz Kurashvili on bass and Vladimir Boldyrev on drums, he swings standards hard and experiments with folk harmonies and phrasings. Two cuts are based on Azerbaijani folk songs with vocals by his wife Elza Mustafa-Zadeh, reminiscent of the Flora Purim-Chick Corea collaboration but transferred to a Turkic cultural milieu.

We cannot know where Vagif Mustafa-Zadeh would have gone had he lived, but two musicians active in Azerbaijan carry on his legacy. Tamaz Kurashvili, whose bass-playing drives the Mustafa-Zadeh album discussed above, has formed a new band and continues to appear at festivals. Aziza Mustafa-Zadeh, the daughter of the Azerbaijani jazzman, is perhaps the brightest new jazz star to appear in the mid-1980s in the Soviet Union. Appearing as both pianist and vocalist for the Rafik Babayev Ensemble from Baku and sometimes as a solo act, she is building on her father's vision of blending jazz and folk harmonies and rhythms.[74]

Other groups with roots in Central Asian music appearing at recent Soviet festivals include Boomerang led by percussionist Takhir Ibraghimov, from Alma Ata, the Grigori Pushen Ensemble and the Semen Morduhaiev Group, both from Tashkent, the David Azarian trio from Yerevan, and the Dustar Group from Bashkiria. In 1987, the Jazz Choral from Tbilisi, Georgia, won a special prize at the International Jazz Vocalist Competition in Poland. The judges were impressed by a repertoire that ranged from Manhattan Transfer standards to indigenous folk material.[75]

Defending the "new jazz" of Ganelin, Kuryokin, and the others Efim Barban wrote that "everything significant and original in jazz music comes out of the avant garde."[76] The Soviet avant garde has caused a sensation, but something of significance is also happening in the southern capitals of the Soviet Union, something that bears a close listening when the opportunity presents itself. Western musicians like John and Alice Coltrane, Ornette Coleman, Yusef Lateef, John McLaughlin, Art Blakey, Rahsaan Roland Kirk, Don Cherry, and others have at one time or another looked to Eastern music, including Islamic music, for inspiration. Soviet musicians do not have to travel to distant lands to find this music. Thanks to the legacy of the imperial empire of the tsars, the Soviet scene is in the unique position of being a "melting pot" where various Islamic or Turkic cultures interact with each other, with the traditional culture of European Russia, and with the American hybrid called jazz.

From our distant vantage point, we cannot predict the evolution of the various tendencies in Soviet jazz. But the vitality and energy of the Soviet scene cannot be denied. Jazz enthusiasts can gain much by listening to Soviet jazz, and musicians should find touring in the Soviet Union a profitable experience. Soviet jazz should also have an impact beyond the music world. It is impossible to think of the Soviet Union in the same way after hearing the music of the Soviet jazz scene and recalling its remarkable history. It is a neglected but potent resource for the important post–Cold War project of rethinking our image of the other superpower.

Notes

I would like to thank Theofanis Stavrou and Reginald Buckner for encouraging me to undertake this project. Several others read drafts, provided materials, and taught by their example: Milo Fine, Colette Hyman, Leigh Kammen, George Lipsitz, Rick Macpherson, Jeff Stewart, and Steve Weiland.

1. Robert Massie, *Peter the Great* (New York: Random House, 1980), 234–39.

2. Nicholas Riasanovsky, "Notes on the Emergence and Nature of the Russian Intelligentsia," in *Art and Culture in Nineteenth-Century Russia*, ed., Theofanis G. Stavrou, (Bloomington: Indiana University Press, 1983), 13.

3. Isaac Deutscher, *Stalin: A Political Biography* 2d ed. (New York: Oxford University Press, 1966), 372.

4. Boris Schwarz, *Music and Musical Life in Soviet Russia: 1917–1983*, enl. ed. (Bloomington: Indiana University Press, 1983), 114.

5. Of course, articles have appeared in the American jazz press from time to time, and careful observers recognized the accomplishments of Soviet jazz musicians long ago. See, for example, Leonard Feather, "Inside Soviet Jazz," *Down Beat*, August 16, 1962, pp. 13–16.

6. In this sense, uncovering the history of Soviet jazz is consistent with the work of the "revisionist" historians and social scientists who have criticized the "totalitarian model" that has dominated Soviet studies in the United States. For them, the Soviet Union is no paradise but certainly more complex than earlier scholarship suggested. Quite likely, Soviet jazz was invisible for so long because the "totalitarian model" encouraged schol-

ars to study the Soviet Union from the top down rather than look for popular initiatives that were assumed nonexistent. For an introduction to the "revisionist" school, see Stephen Cohen, *Rethinking the Soviet Experience* (New York: Oxford University Press, 1985).

7. Frederick Starr, *Red and Hot: The Fate of Jazz in the Soviet Union* (New York: Oxford University Press, 1983).

8. Starr, 43–55.

9. Starr, 62ff.

10. Starr, 85.

11. Starr, 89ff.

12. Starr, chap. 7.

13. Starr, 183ff.

14. Starr, 194ff.

15. Starr, 225.

16. Starr, 226ff.

17. Starr, 236ff.

18, Starr, 271.

19. Starr, 275, 282.

20. Starr, 285.

21. Alexey Batashev, *Sovetskii Dzhaz: istoricheskii ocherk* (Soviet Jazz: A Historical Sketch) (Moscow, 1972). Apparently, more than half the original manuscript was cut by the censors before publication, especially passages mentioning the earlier repression of jazz and the emigration of jazz musicians to the United States (Starr, 305). Still, there is much of value here.

22. Leonid Pereversev, "Dzhaz," *Bolshaya sovetskaya entsiklopedia* 3d ed. (1972) 8: 539–40; and in English translation: "Jazz," *Great Soviet Encyclopedia*, 3d ed. (New York: Macmillan, 1973–1982) 8: 548. For a more in-depth analysis by the same author, see "Dzhaz," *Muzykalnaya entsiklopedia* (Moscow, 1974) 2: 211–19.

23. *Jazzman* (My iz dzhaza), directed by Karen Shakhnazarov, screenplay by Shaknazarov and Alexander Borodyansky, music by Anatoly Kroll and his Sovremennik Orchestra, produced by Mosfilm in 1983, released through International Film Exchange, Ltd. One American jazz critic compared it favorably to *Round Midnight*, writing that *Jazzman* has "more feeling for the subversive and communal mysteries of a music that often chooses to stand on the outskirts of respectability" than the French jazz film. Gary Giddins, "For Jazz—With Love and Squalor," *Village Voice*, October 14, 1986, p. 86.

24. Larissa Dolina is in fact a respected jazz vocalist whom the leading Soviet jazz critic has called "the strongest voice on the Soviet jazz scene." She may also be a good actor, but this was not her role. See Alexey Batashev, "Autumn Rhythms '86," *Jazz Forum*, 104 (1987): 18. *Jazz Forum* is the bimonthly magazine of the International Jazz Federation. It is published in English and Polish editions at Warsaw. Subscriptions available

through East Wind Trade Associates, 3325 17th St. NW, Washington, D.C. 20010.

25. Starr, 292ff.

26. Official bands like Time Machine and the Stas Namin group play slick power pop and draw big crowds to arena concerts. Meanwhile there is a thriving "underground" of unofficial rock bands that express youthful rebellion by assembling images of alienation from the hippie, heavy metal, and punk repertoires and coding their messages in "poetic" lyrics. A sampling of these bands can be heard on the album *Red Wave: Four Underground Bands from the U.S.S.R.*.

In 1987, glasnost came to underground Soviet Rock. Aquarium, the best-known underground band, recorded for Melodiya, crossing the line into respectability, and then signed a contract with CBS Records. For background, see Naomi Marcus, "Glasnost's First Gold Record," *Mother Jones*, October 1988, 30–31; Michael R. Benson, "Rock in Russia," *Rolling Stone*, March 26, 1987, p. 15; and Artemy Troitsky, *Back in the USSR: The True Story of Rock in Russia* (London: Omnibus, 1987). Troitsky, Moscow's most famous rock critic, organized the Chernobyl aid concert.

27. Soviet records are available in the United States primarily through East Wind Records and Leo Records. Leo Records is run by Leo Feigen, a Soviet emigré who has issued a full catalog of Soviet and East European jazz, much of it based on bootleg tapes and most of it avant garde. East Wind began in 1986 by reissuing five records originally produced in the Soviet Union, including work by Arsenel, Igor Brill, the Ganelin Trio, Vagif Mustafa-Zadeh, and Alexey Kuznetsov. See the discography (Appendix B) for all records mentioned in the text.

28. Among the hundreds of quality players in the USSR, some of the best known groups are Kadans (Cadence), led by trumpeter German Lukyanov, who has been a key figure in the Moscow scene since the 1950s; Nikolai Levinovski's Allegro, which featured the tenor sax of Igor Butman, a man in his twenties who fronted a student band at the 1984 Moscow festival, quickly became a dominant force at this instrument and is now an emigré, the Victor Budarin Octet from Novosibirsk, Siberia; the Mikhail Okun Trio; the Leningrad duo of Vyacheslav Gayvoronsky (trumpet) and Vladimir Volkov (bass), who are somewhere between bop and free; the Moscow Saxophone Quartet, featuring Alexander Oseichuk, who is well known from his work with Igor Brill; and from Estonia, the Arvo Pilliroog Ensemble and the trio of Tonu Naissoo, who is the son of the now deceased Uno Naissoo, the famous Estonian jazz composer.

Many musicians have independent reputations as soloists: for example, Leonid Chizhik, an eclectic pianist originally from Kharkov but now based in Moscow, whose work ranges from lyrical covers of Alexander Tsfasman's hits to avant garde collaborations; Alexei Zubov, whose tenor sax work is another long-time institution in Soviet jazz; and multitalented

David Goloshchekin, a fixture of the Leningrad scene. A rising star is Lithuanian reedman Petras Vishnyauskas, the protégé of Vladimir Chekasin; like his teacher, he plays in many styles and combinations. Finally, there are the vocalists, especially Larissa Dolina, Tatevik Oganesyan, Elvina Makarian, and the new phenomenon, Aziza Mustafa-Zadeh.

29. Starr, 314. For general background, see Tatiana Didenko, "Arsenel: Ever in Quest of New Discoveries," *Music in the USSR*, July–August 1986, 74–77. Arsenel has released four records on the Melodiya label.

30. See Starr, 256ff, for the big band revival, and 226–257, on the Oleg Lundstrem band. Besides Lundstrem's band, the most respected Soviet big band in the 1960s was the Yosif Weinstein band, which featured Gennadi Goldstein. Current big bands include the Kim Nazavetov Big Band from Rostov-on-Don. The omnipresent Vladimir Chekasin's experimental big band, composed of musicians from Vilnius, Lithuania, can be heared (and should be heard) on the album *New Vitality* (Leo 142).

31. See Starr, 252, for the Dixieland revival. The Leningrad Dixieland Jazz Band toured the United States in 1987. Among other well-known Dixielanders are the Seven Simeons, composed of the seven Ovechkin brothers from Irkutsk, Siberia. G.M., "The Seven Magnificent," *Jazz Forum* 101 (1986): 25–26.

32. Vladimir Feiertag, "Augumn Rhythms '85: A Jazz Festival in Leningrad," *Music in the USSR* (April–May 1986), 84.

33. Starr, 308; Alexey Batashev, "Moscow Jazz Festival: Business as Usual," *Jazz Forum* 90 (1984): 26. For a report on the Fifth Tallinn Student Jazz Festival (1987), see Valtar Ojakaar, "Estonian Jazz Flash," *Jazz Forum* 109 (1987): 9–10.

34. Alexey Batashev, "Professionals and Winners," *Jazz Forum* 100 (1986): 17–18.

35. Joachim E. Berendt, *The Jazz Book: From Ragtime to Fusion and Beyond*, transl. H. and B. Bredikeit with Dan Morgenstern (Westport: Lawrence Hill, 1982), 383.

36. "Filmmakers Eye Problems, Debate Reforms," *Current Digest of the Soviet Press*, June 18, 1986, p. 383.

37. "Voznesensky, Yevtushenko Address Writers," *Current Digest of the Soviet Press*, August 13, 1986, pp. 1–3, 15.

38. Alexei Batashev, "Takefiving Brubeck in Unsquare USSR," *Jazz Forum* 108 (1987): 22–23.

39. Alexey Batashev, "Jazz on the Wing," *Jazz Forum* 107 (1987): 15–16.

40. Antero Pietila, "Composer, producer busy pushing rock music in the USSR," *Minneapolis Star Tribune*, March 19, 1988, p. 6E.

41. Pawel Brodowski, "The Tbilisi Earthquake," *Jazz Forum* 103 (1986): 43. Yevgeny Machavariani, "Tbilisi '86," *Music in the USSR* (Oct.–Dec., 1986), 6–9.

42. Alexander Medvedev, "Vvedeniye: Vremya zrelosti" (Introduction: The Age of Maturity), in *Sovetskii Dzhaz: Problemy, Sobytiva, Mastera*, ed. Alexander and Olga Medvedev (Soviet Jazz: Problems, Events, Masters) (Moscow, 1987), 37. This book is a 600-page anthology of writings about jazz, especially during the period from 1960 to 1982. It includes theoretical articles, profiles of Soviet musicians, reviews of Soviet books on jazz, and a discography of Soviet jazz records.

43. For example, the Ganelin Trio was voted the top combo in the European category by the readers of *Jazz Forum* in the Twentieth Annual Top People Poll; *Jazz Forum* 104 (1987): 4–6.

44. Alan Bookbinder, Olivia & Denton, *Comrades: Portraits of Soviet Life* (New York: New American Library, 1985), 158–71. This book was prepared by the producers of the BBC series by the same name.

45. Leo Feigen, "Siberian Jazz," in *Russian Jazz: New Identity*, ed. Leo Feigen, (London: Quartet, 1985), 112–20.

46. Alexey Batashev, "Moscow Jazz Fest: Business as Usual," *Jazz Forum* 90 (1984): 26; Bert Noglik, "Arkhangelsk, Arkhangelsk," in *Russian Jazz*, 85–97.

47. Virgil Mihaiu, "Prophets of New Horizons," in *Russian Jazz*, 44–60; originally published as "Ganelin Trio: Prophetic Vision," in *Jazz Forum* 91 (1984): 30–36. Howard Mandel, "The Ganelin Trio: Jazz Detente," *Down Beat*, September 1986, 26.

48. Pawel Brodowski, "The Tbilisi Earthquake," *Jazz Forum* 103 (1986): 43. Adam Baruch, "Ganelin Arrival," *Jazz Forum* 111 (1988): 21–22.

49. Virgil Mihaiu, "Vladimir Tarasov: an all-round percussionist," *Jazz Forum* 109 (1987): 36–39, 46–47.

50. Mihaiu, "Prophets of New Horizon," 53–54.

51. These impressions are based on their performance at Ruby's Nightclub in Minneapolis, during their 1986 tour.

52. Steve Boulay, "Soviet Trio Swings America," *Jazz Forum* 103 (1986): 38–42. This article contains a sampling of critical commentary on the Ganelin performances. Serge Schememann, "The Ganelin Trio Come To Town for a Night of Jazz to a Soviet Beat," *New York Times*, June 20, 1986, p. C22.

53. Quoted in Boulay, 40.

54. Gary Giddins, "JVC Jazz Festival: The Mixture as Before," *Village Voice*, July 22, 1986, p. 72.

55. Jon Pareles, "Ganelin Trio Debut," *New York Times*, June 23, 1986.

56. Michael Jarrett and Michael Desch, "Russia," *Jazziz*, (Oct.–Nov. 1986), 42.

57. Feigen, "Introduction," in *Russian Jazz*, 1. Two book reviews, both very critical, can be found at *Down Beat*, August 1987, 55–56 (Bill Shoemaker), and *Jazz Forum* 103 (1986): 56–58 (Adam Baruch).

58. Efim Barban, "Soviet Jazz: New Identity," in *Russian Jazz*, 20.

59. Mihaiu, "Prophets of New Horizon," 52.

60. Kuryokin interview, "Ways of Freedom," 107.

61. Berendt, 11.

62. John Rockwell, *All American Music: Composition in the Later Twentieth Century*, (New York: Knopf, 1983), 192.

63. Feigen, "Introduction," in *Russian Jazz*, 2.

64. Ralph S. Clem, "Ethnicity," in *Soviet Union Today*, ed. James Cracraft, 2d ed. (Chicago: University of Chicago Press, 1988), 303–314.

65. Michael Kaufman, "The East Bloc Tolerates Jazz But Mutes its Dissident Note," *New York Times*, January 4, 1986, p. C1.

66. Alexander Medvedev, "Vvedeniye: Vremya zrelosti," 41.

67. Frederick Starr, "Soviet Jazz: The Third Wave," in *Russian Jazz*, 4.

68. Alexey Batashev, *Sovetskii Dzhaz: Istoricheskii Ockerk* (Moscow: 1972), 158.

69. Alexander Medvedev, 44.

70. Quoted in Batashev, 159.

71. Quoted in Batashev, 162.

72. Virgil Mihaiu, "A 1984 Panorama of Soviet Jazz," in *Russian Jazz*, 154–71, 162.

73. Ibid., 160–63; Alexey Batashev and Igor Kosolobenkov, "Vostochnyi dzhaz Vagifa Mustafy-zade," (The Eastern Jazz of Vagif Mustafa-Zade) in *Sovetskii Dzhaz*, 290–95.

74. Pawel Brodowski, "The Tbilisi Earthquake," 45; Howard Mandel, "The State of Jazz in the Soviet Union," *Down Beat*, September 1986, 56, 63.

75. Andrej Schmidt, "Vocal Tournament," *Jazz Forum* 109 (1987): 7–8.

76. Barban, 14.

The PROBLEM of
LOCAL JAZZ HISTORY:
The EXAMPLE of
SOUTH CAROLINA

Benjamin Franklin V

When, in 1955, Horizon Press published the first volume of Leonard Feather's monumental *Encyclopedia of Jazz*, jazz fans rejoiced. At last, all agreed, a book offered what everyone wanted: a fairly comprehensive listing of the major jazz musicians, with pertinent personal and professional information, in addition to an occasional judgment about their music. In time, the increasing number of musicians necessitated an enlarged edition (1960), another edition (1966), and yet another (coauthored by Ira Gitler). If only because the last, published over a decade ago, includes no musician, alphabetically, between Marty Marsala and Wayne Marsh, a fourth volume is needed. But for all the numerous and obvious strengths of Feather's books, they are neither error-free nor all-inclusive. No book is perfect (is anything?); Leon Edel's biographical studies of Henry James—to use an example of biographical exhaustiveness from another field—doubtless omit material that would interest someone. Furthermore, while Feather includes information about many musicians, he does not mention, probably because of space limitations, numerous minor or fringe musicians who have recorded infrequently, if at all, but who have made their own modest contributions to the music and are as dedicated to it as are the famous players who have, usually, recorded frequently. And to defend Feather in another way, recordings are, on one level, a measure of a musician's importance.

Discography offers another approach to documenting musicians' careers. This mysterious, valuable art details all the facts one cares to know about recording sessions. (Is that Anita O'Day or Alice B. Toklas, the choices the liner notes offer, singing "Fall Out" on *Jazz Surprise* [Crown CLP 5008]? O'Day is obviously the vocalist, but even if the listener is uncertain, some discographer has the answer, although no discographer mentioned below or O'Day herself in *Hard Times Hard Times*, her autobiography, mentions the recording.) The master contemporary discographers—those who have attempted to be more comprehensive than the others—are Brian Rust, Jorgen Grunnet Jepsen, and Walter Bruyninckx, non-Americans all. (The first real discographer was the Frenchman Charles Delaunay, who published the first serious discography in 1948.) Although they include blues musicians, they focus on jazz performers. The first has documented jazz recordings through 1942; the second, since 1941; the third, *all* jazz recordings. To these researchers' credit, they are inclusive, not exclusive. For example, the South Carolina pianist Al (Stomp) Russell apparently recorded only once—with Timmy Rogers in 1945—but once is enough. Because of this one session, he is important to discographers, as Bruyninckx's index attests. And artist discographies—those about one musician (Sun Ra, Stan Getz)—which Europeans, especially, are producing at an astonishing rate, regularly include recording information that the more comprehensive discographers have missed. The more specialized one's interest, the more accurate and complete one can be.

No matter how many volumes of the *Encyclopedia* Leonard Feather or any successors might publish, or how many additions Walter Bruyninckx makes to his *60 Years of Recorded Jazz*, their research will be, despite its unquestioned usefulness, incomplete. The best way to document—and by document I mean to gather material about, not evaluate or interpret—jazz and blues musicians most completely, I am convinced, is to do so at the local level. The facts of the major performers' lives and careers are well documented, although more can always be done with them, as James Lincoln Collier's curious books on Louis Armstrong and Duke Ellington attest; generally speaking only the locals who care about the middling and minor players are in a position to collect material about them. If all localities would document their improvising musicians—possibly by large city and state in the United States and by country elsewhere—the findings might then be submitted to a central agency that would house the information in what would amount to an international archives and clearinghouse. A model for distributing information might be the Online Computer Library Center (OCLC), which provides information about books to libraries. But this is presently the ideal, or possibly it is only my ideal. In the interim, between now and the realization of this dream, should it ever occur, let the local enthusiasts begin inquiring, interviewing, and collecting while the old timers are still living and while the tyros are striving to be heard.

Immediately upon moving from Michigan to Columbia, South Carolina, in 1976, I noticed that in the state capital, which is also the state's largest city, jazz and blues were unavailable, either live or on the local radio stations; that finding jazz or blues records locally was almost impossible; and that few people—not even students at the state's largest university, where I teach—knew about or cared to learn about jazz or blues. This is top-forty and country country. Lack of live music, my inability to keep abreast of new recordings, and the lack of people to talk with about jazz and blues discouraged me. But how do I account for the general lack of interest in listening to and learning about South Carolina's most creative musicians? We have known at least since the time of Christ how citizens value their prophets, but with such Charlie Parker and Ornette Coleman compositions as "Confirmation" and "Lonely Woman" being heard in elevators, and with such tunes as "Flat Floot Floogie" being played in Turkish airplanes—I heard it on a Turkish plane in 1983—surely jazz, to illustrate the point, is no longer the arcane music that bop was in the 1940s or that free jazz was in the late 1950s and early 1960s, although Slim Gaillard might still seem far out to the unhip. Vout? So the question about the lack of interest in jazz and blues musicians remains, for me, unanswered, although I suspect that the answer has something to do with most people's desire for the predictable and comfortable rather than the experimental.

After accepting the fact that few people care about the musicians I admire, I began working to make available information about these musicians, should anyone become interested in them. But first I had to inform myself. Because I knew that the Southeast had produced many blues musicians, I assumed that some must have been South Carolinians, although I could not name one who had been. In time, I discovered that Josh White was a South Carolinian (from Greenville), as were Pink Anderson (Spartanburg), Reverend Gary Davis (Laurens), Scrapper Blackwell (probably born in Syracuse), and others. While I like the blues, I love jazz, so I made similar inquiries about these musicians I listen to most frequently. I soon found that the Cheraw native Dizzy Gillespie—the only musician I knew for certain had come from South Carolina—is, surprisingly, merely the most famous of many South Carolina jazz musicians, and that some of them—such as Blood Ulmer (from St. Matthews), Bubber Miley (Aiken), and Jabbo Smith (reared at the Jenkins Orphanage in Charleston)—have made significant contributions to the music. I even discovered that Smith, whom I had thought long dead, was not only alive, but that he had shared an engagement at the Village Vanguard with trumpeter Don Cherry in 1987.

I wanted to document thoroughly the South Carolina jazz and blues musicians. This meant identifying them, establishing their discographies, contacting them, and interviewing them. Before I began, I arranged with the University of South Carolina's Caroliniana Library to house, in what would be called the South Carolina Jazz and Blues Archives, all the material I would collect. At the beginning of my research, I knew not what to expect. Would I find a dozen musicians, or hundreds?

I had to confront immediately two seemingly simple but actually difficult questions, both having to do with inclusivity. First, what is a jazz or a blues musician? I could not then answer this question, nor can I now, with much confidence. Finally, I decided that, obviously, such musicians play jazz or blues music, but I also have difficulty defining these terms, and they perform with others who are usually described as jazz or blues musicians. This definition, while doubtless inadequate in other contexts, allowed me to proceed with my research without worrying unduly about who is and who is not a jazz or a blues musician or what jazz and blues are. For example, even though Johnny Williams (Orangeburg) calls himself a "recreative musician"—he does not improvise—his years of playing baritone saxophone with the Count Basie band easily qualify him for inclusion as a jazz musician, according to my definition. And Irene Daye (Greenville)? Because she sang with Gene Krupa for over two years, immediately preceding Anita O'Day as Krupa's female vocalist, she is a jazz musician. Eartha Kitt (North) and Brook Benton (Camden)? Because they are or were primarily popular singers—even though Benton's roots were obviously in the blues —and because they do not or did not usually perform with jazz or blues musicians, others must chronicle their careers.

The second troubling question was this: What is a South Carolinian? After grappling with it for longer than I care to admit, I determined that a South Carolinian is one who (1) was born in the state, (2) was reared here, or (3) chose to reside here. In other words, the definition is so inclusive that I might document musicians that researchers in other states, if there are others engaged in a project similar to mine, might also be documenting. So be it. Because of this definition, I consider as South Carolinians all the musicians who lived, for however long, at the Jenkins Orphanage, regardless of where they were born. Among them, Tommy Benford was born in West Virginia; Jabbo Smith, Georgia; Peanuts Holland, Virginia; and Ermitt V. Perry, Florida. Some musicians were born elsewhere but chose as adults to live in South Carolina—North Carolinian Nappy Brown, who lives in Pomaria; Georgian Sam Gary, who lived in Aiken; and Illinoisan Jack Howe, who lives in Chapin; and therefore they are, to me, South Carolinians.

While I am interested in all South Carolina jazz and blues musicians, I am especially interested in those who have recorded, those whose contributions to music can be demonstrated by listening to something they have played. For this reason, I am presently more interested in Al (Stomp) Russell than in Rex O'Steen. Russell recorded once, apparently; O'Steen, born in Kentucky but a long-time resident of Greenville, probably did not record, although he played lead trombone in Glenn Millers' Air Force band in 1942. (Whether the Miller band should be categorized as jazz is another question.) If I can find Miller recordings or airchecks on which O'Steen appears, he will then likely become of primary interest to me. I am also charting musicians who are at the beginning of their careers. Freddy Vanderford, resident of Union and leader of a group called The Shades, is one such musician. His group is about to make its first recording. Because Vanderford and such others as Delbert Felix (from Beaufort, who is presently with Branford Marsalis and has recorded with Felix) know about the archives, they and other young musicians will, I hope, cooperate in documenting their careers. Thus, years from now we will possibly have a fairly complete file on the Vanderfords and Felixes, who by then might well have become as significant as Peg Leg Sam from Jonesville or Jimmy Hamilton from Union.

Identifying the South Carolina musicians is an ongoing process. To date, I have identified approximately 130 of them. Some I identified by consulting standard reference works, such as Feather's *Encyclopedia*. Less accessible reference works also proved valuable, including John Chilton's indispensable *A Jazz Nursery: The Story of the Jenkins' Orphanage Bands*, a pamphlet published by the Bloomsbury Book Shop in London in 1980 and previously unknown to me or to the librarians at the Caroliniana Library. Tommy Benford, who was reared in the orphanage and who had assisted Chilton during his research, was the first to tell me about Chilton's seminal work. My associate Tom Johnson, of the Caroliniana Library, sent to every newspaper in the state a letter requesting assistance in identifying South Carolina's jazz and blues musicians. The letter generated a good response, including that from Rex O'Steen. It also led to my learning, from a 1986 obituary provided by a newspaper editor, that Sam Gary had lived his last twenty years or so in South Carolina. Musicians led me to other musicians; serendipity occasionally came into play.

Almost all the South Carolina musicians I have contacted have been cooperative. Only one that I asked for an interview was less than accommodating: he granted me the interview but would not permit me to tape it. Others, Blood Ulmer and Jimmy Hamilton among them, have proven elusive, although I have come close to reaching Ulmer on two occasions and Hamilton once. And locating some of them has involved considerable detective work. Finding Webster Young, from Columbia, demanded the most sleuthing. Frankly, I thought him dead, if only because his recording career stopped abruptly after a year of fairly frequent recording in the 1950s. How could someone who played as well as he did with the likes of Jackie McLean and John Coltrane and who had his own session for Prestige disappear without a trace? I tried to locate him but was prepared to be disappointed. In desperation, I wrote to the two men who had offered to advise me on this project. I asked if either of them could help me locate some missing musicians, one of whom was Young. Michael Ullman, the Boston jazz critic, responded by return mail: Young lives in Washington, D.C. How did he know? Because Young's son is a student at Tufts University, where Ullman teaches, and Ullman knows the son or knows of him.

Ullman gave me Young's address, I contacted the trumpeter, and we had an excellent three-hour talk at Young's home. Not all searching has led to such a pleasant conclusion. After finally discovering the telephone number of the Charleston native Freddie Green, I called him. "Mr. Green?" I asked. Green's son, who had answered the phone, told me that his father had died three days earlier.

Of the interviews I have conducted, twelve—with Tommy Benford, Nappy Brown, Ron Free, Dizzy Gillespie, Jack Howe, Etta Jones, Horace Ott, Houston Person, Arthur Prysock, Jabbo Smith, Johnny Williams, and Webster Young—have been edited for broadcast on the South Carolina Educational Radio Network. The programs will become part of the archives. The interviews are also being prepared for book publication. The reason for so disseminating this material, aside from its inherent interest, is to publicize the archives and these musicians—only Gillespie is widely known. The better known the archives, the more likely musicians will wish to be associated with it. Popularity breeds popularity; success, success. If the musicians cooperate, as they have done so far, the archives might someday contain fairly comprehensive information about many South Carolina jazz and blues musicians. Until then, I—and, I hope, my successors, if any—will continue documenting the state's most creative musicians. If such a resource can be created in South Carolina—and it is a big if—so can one be elsewhere: in New York, in Canada, in Poland, in Greece. Once this local research begins to proliferate and is disseminated through, ideally, a central agency, it will permit writers, scholars, and other interested parties to comment more intelligently than previously about jazz and blues musicians because they will then have access to most of what is known about these musicians, including musicians' recollections of recordings that discographers have not yet discovered. Performances by Jabbo Smith reside unreleased in the hands of a Dutch collector, for example.

Central to all this are the less exalted musicians with whom even the initiated are generally unfamiliar. Because they never became great artists or known to the public does not mean that their lives in music are unimportant. Often these lesser lights offer profound insights into the musical life precisely because they have had to scuffle. Drink Small, from Bishopville and a resident of Columbia, has not had an easy time making a living as a blues singer. Because he has had little success in interesting recording companies in his music, twice he has released his own singles. Frank

Motley, from Cheraw, has released a single of his own music. Unlike Drink Small, the tenor saxophonist Jack Howe has not attempted to make a living from music and has been successful in other areas; yet, he is important to a jazz researcher: he has played improvised music for sixty years. As a member of the Princeton Triangle Club Jazz Band in 1928, he participated in one of the earliest recording sessions by a college jazz group. He tells an amusing story about almost having recorded with his acquaintance Bix Beiderbecke. Some collectors covet those Bix-less recordings because Bix intended to be on them. Howe participated in the Chicago jazz scene during the late 1920s and early 1930s, and, because for nineteen years he lived in Evanston at Squirrel Ashcraft's House of Jazz, he played with and got to know well many Chicago jazz musicians and those who passed through Chicago. There are other Jack Howes—relatively unknown musicians whose lives in music parallel and augment the lives of well-known jazz and blues performers. Local jazz and blues fans, historians, and archivists are in the best position to discover and preserve these musicians' stories, and they must do so.

The local researcher must be careful, however. Interviews, or oral histories, as they are called euphemistically, do not constitute hard research. The information gained from an interview must be verified by other sources that have been proven reliable. Even the most honest, most lucid, and most mnemonically acute musician will get carried away with his narrative, misremember, or remember not at all. Because Tommy Benford and Jabbo Smith cannot recall many details about their experiences at the Jenkins Orphanage does not mean that they were not there, that their experiences were not valuable, or that either has mental problems. When I spoke with Benford, he was eighty-two years old; Smith was probably seventy-nine. Memory fades. Furthermore, because Smith has difficulty speaking, Lorraine Gordon and I had to recreate and interpret words before I could provide a transcript of the interview. Therefore, the researcher using my interviews with Benford and Smith as primary documents must be careful not to make unwarranted inferences. (A transcriber's editorial principles constitute another area of needed critical discussion.)

The arranger Horace Ott, from St. Matthews, has had numerous successes, including arranging the all-black production of *Guys and Dolls*. Yet, during our interview he recalled the critic Clive Barnes writing in the *New York Times* about Ott's arrangements for *Dude* in this manner: Barnes "stated something like, 'those arrangements are fantastic. Horace Ott put sounds in the Broadway theater that have never been there before, but should always be there.'" In fact, Barnes does not mention Ott, although he comments, on October 10, 1972, about the music in *Dude*: "the show's major thrust rests on Galt MacDermott's music—loud, strident, over-amplified and yet often effectively powerful." Was Ott inaccurate? Certainly. Did he lie? No. Did he elaborate on the truth? Maybe, but maybe not. He was speaking to someone who wanted to learn as much as possible about him, and putting one's best face forward is human nature. He accommodated me. Ott is a pleasure to speak with: he is enthusiastic about music and, while not boastful, he is not reluctant to discuss his accomplishments, which are numerous. He made the *Dude* reference in the context of his achievements; he did not have with him a copy of Barnes's review. But even though he misremembered, in mentioning Barnes's review he gave me the lead I needed to discover what Barnes really wrote. How many of us recall the details of something relatively unimportant that happened fifteen years earlier? Not many.

Again, I wish to encourage the local jazz and blues fans to become researchers, although they must be careful. But even if they are relatively uninformed, do not validate an interviewee's every point, and do not correct mistakes, the interviews are still valuable. They are documents that someone possibly better trained than the interviewer can use cautiously as a means of learning about musicians. Interviews at least record information that others can work with. If only someone had interviewed Al (Stomp) Russell.

The QUOTER and HIS CULTURE

Krin Gabbard

Soloing on a 1949 recording of "Body and Soul," saxophonist James Moody cites Percy Grainger's "Country Gardens" by briefly quoting an easily recognized phrase.[1] With this playful, seemingly simple reference Moody may have been paying tribute to the composer and his music even if at that moment he could recall the name of neither Grainger nor his composition. It is more likely, however, that he was alluding not to Grainger but to Charlie Parker and other members of the bebop movement who frequently quoted the song. By 1948 Parker had adopted the regular practice of concluding a selection with a brief coda derived from the melody of "Country Gardens."[2] Although all artists—even jazz musicians—can never be completely original, Moody's quotation may also be conceptualized as a short respite from the demands of creating "new" phrases as the solo develops. Relying on the work of Barry Kernfeld, we might compare the quoting jazz artist to an oral poet, who recites a few lines of well-established formulas before composing a line requiring more originality.[3]

There is the additional possibility that Moody was sharing a joke with the hipsters in his audience who could appreciate the intrusion into a soulful jazz ballad of the punctillious music of a white bourgeois drawing room (or a black bourgeois drawing room, where jazz could be just as unlikely.) At the same time, he may have been "signifying" on Grainger as well as on the squares in his audience, who could most enjoy his complex music only when a familiar tune passed by.[4] As this interpretation suggests, the art of quotation provides the jazz artist with modes of expression that are otherwise blocked by forces based in race, class, and popular taste. In the hands of the beboppers, the practice became what I call an "avant-garde gesture," not unlike disruptions of classical art in the European vanguard movements of the early twentieth century. Like their predecessors in this "historical avant garde," boppers used quotation to undermine distinctions between high and low art and to question the "aura" that in the minds of most listeners surrounds the work of composers like Percy Grainger but not the improvisations of a black saxophone player. In addition, the quoting bop artist creates the effect of a collage, something that Peter Burger has called a "fundamental principle of avant-gardiste art."[5] Although the term "avant-garde jazz" has most commonly been associated with the "free" music of Ornette Coleman, Cecil Taylor, and their followers in the 1960s, I would suggest that bebop and free jazz share an avant-garde character, especially when they employ quotation and other collage effects.

The art of quotation in jazz did not, of course, originate in the bop era. In 1929, when Louis Armstrong cited Gershwin's "Rhapsody in Blue" during his solo on "Ain't Misbehavin'" he was probably paying tribute to Gershwin in much the same way that a classical composer might honor a predecessor.[6] Even when Armstrong quoted from advertizing jingles, he probably intended for the audience to join him in the pleasant surprise of hearing a familiar melody performed in an unfamiliar context. Although Armstrong was capable of expressing ambivalence toward his role in American culture, he almost certainly thought of himself primarily as an entertainer.[7] Without denying the trumpet player's brilliance as an improviser, we can generalize that in comparison with bop quoters his use of quotation was less complicated by conflicting messages.

By the late 1930s and early 1940s, Lester Young may have been quoting with a little more irony, probably providing the inspiration for a good deal of bop quoting. The self-effacing Young—who often spoke in his own evasive, highly coded language—never made grandiose claims for his creative genius. Nevertheless, the musician likely saw himself as more artist than entertainer.[8] He was also deeply aware of the extent to which racial prejudice undermined his acceptance as an artist. For a public that would not or could not hear his music as he might have wished, Young would pepper his improvisations, perhaps mockingly, with brief allusions to pop ephemera ("Sing for Your Supper"), to songs with a racist inflection ("All God's Children Got Rhythm"), or to a repertoire associated predominantly with white jazz groups ("My Sweetie Went Away").

In their solos, bebop artists often referred to the same kinds of music as Young, but when a bopper such as Moody quotes from "Country Gardens" in the middle of "Body and Soul," the gesture is consistent with the new consciousness that made the bop ear possible. As Gary Giddins has pointed out, musicians like Parker, Moody, Dizzy Gillespie, and Thelonius Monk were born during the Harlem Renaissance, and their music "set the most comprehensive tone for black discontent and black accomplishment."[9] By juxtaposing a light classical ditty with one of the most familiar melodies in jazz, Moody fragments the audience in a way that an older artist such as Armstrong would never have intended: some will miss the reference altogether (a bopper is never likely to dwell on a quotation for long); others will hear it and recognize it in the same spirit that they might recognize Armstrong's quotation of "Rhapsody in Blue." And a select group of initiates will catch the irony of a black jazz artist dipping into the sedate repertoire of a completely different milieu. Usually playing with poker faces, Moody and his peers indicate no visible preference for any one of these three groups. A desire to join the aficionados may impel some prehip members of the audience to reconsider their role in a culture that regards Percy Grainger as more worthy than Charlie Parker. Indeed, the hip posture of bop era musicians—who found elaborate strategies for negotiating their ambiguous contract with American culture—has had a substantial role in defining the spirit of alienation that characterizes much American art since the 1950s. The Beat movement and, to a large extent, the Hippie movement would not have been possible without the direct or indirect influence of performance practices originating with bop.[10]

In this sense, jazz since the 1940s has helped change the coinage of American art and its reception just as earlier avant-garde movements once sought to alter European art. Although every epoch has had its rebels, Europe in the first decades of this century saw the rise of "alienated" artists. In the words of Matei Calinescu, an eminent critic of modernist movements, these artists "felt the need to disrupt and completely overthrow the whole bourgeois system of values, with all its philistine pretensions to universality."[11] Polemicists for the period's more notorious movements proposed entirely new means of thinking about art and the world. Surrealism sought a greater truth in the terrain of the unconscious, which Sigmund Freud was then charting. The Futurists called for the destruction of all museums and libraries and reveled in the aesthetics of war. The Dadaist poet Tzara suggested cutting words out of a newspaper, pulling the scraps randomly out of a hat, and then presenting the resulting poem as evidence that one is "an author of charming sensibility."[12] The most famous avant-garde work of art from this period is probably Marcel Duchamp's *Fountain by R. Mutt* of 1917. Appropriating a urinal, signing it, and then placing it within a museum carries most of what seems essential to avant-garde art: the goal of "épater les bourgeois" is satisfied; older traditions are ignored or desecrated with what Calinescu calls "deliberately stupid humor" (p. 125); and the entire process by which art gains its legitimacy is questioned.

Not surprisingly, the artists of the historical avant-garde were attracted to jazz if only because the music offended the pre-World War I guardians of high culture. Although most regularly wood-shedding jazz artists have a good idea of what they will play before and during a solo, many European avant-gardistes believed that improvising artists created with complete spontaneity. Especially in the minds of the Surrealists, black jazz artists had succeeded in finding a direct route to the unconscious without first having to consult ideological manifestoes.[13] One of the great artistic scandals of the twentieth century's second decade was at least partially related to the injection of jazz into the musty, respectable domain of ballet. Stravinsky had already provoked a French audience into throwing chairs during the legendary 1913 premiere of his *Le Sacre du Printemps*, with its primitive, African-sounding rhythms. The first concert treatment of jazz in French music was the opening performance of Erik Satie's 1917 ballet *Parade*, for which Jean Cocteau had written the scenario and Picasso had designed Cubist sets and costumes. In *Parade* Satie, who had been drawn to jazz as a music that "shouts its sorrows," mixed Afro-American sounds with music originally scored for sirens, typewriters, airplane propellers, and a lottery wheel. In the program notes for *Parade*, Guillaume Apollinaire used the word "surrealism" for the first time.[14] Audiences were properly scandalized. At this time, the presence of the slightest jazz inflection in a bourgeois concert hall was as shocking and provocative as a Duchamp Ready-Made.

There are major differences between the world of the prewar European avant-garde and the music of Taylor and Coleman that has been called avant-garde jazz. Most important, the substantial distance that has always existed between jazz and high art makes the old avant-garde stance unavailable to the contemporary jazz artist. Originally produced at the lowest strata of society, and still associated today with prostitution and drug addiction, jazz has never possessed the "aura" that Walter Benjamin identifies in his seminal 1935 essay, "The Work of Art in the Age of Mechanical Reproduction."[15]

Writing about the radically different ways that audiences experience movies as opposed to the painting and sculpture enshrined in museums, Benjamin argues that the works of the Old Masters are the natural inheritors of the sacred qualities that gave religious art an aura, that is, an air of unapproachability, or a "unique phenomenon of distance, however close it may be" (Benjamin, 222). A photograph of a painting, like the print of a motion picture, does not possess this kind of an aura and can more effectively be understood on its own terms. Benjamin (237–38) credits the Dadaists with creating the same effect in their own works:

> The Dadaists attached much less importance to the sales value of their work than to its uselessness for contemplative immersion. The studied degradation of their material was not the least of their means to achieve this uselessness. Their poems are "word salad" containing obscenities and every imaginable waste product of language. The same is true of their paintings, on which they mounted buttons and tickets. What they intended and achieved was a relentless destruction of the aura of their creations, which they branded as reproductions with the very means of production.

Unfortunately, Benjamin does not discuss the process by which music acquires an aura. If anything, the mechanical reproduction of a piece of music can inspire greater awe than the original, which does not, of course, exist only as an unchanging collection of staff paper. The sound of a Beethoven sonata performed this week by a relatively unknown pianist in a concert hall does not have the same aura as a scratchy 1932 recording of the same pieces performed by a legendary figure like Artur Schnabel. For many Beethoven lovers, Schnabel's recordings are still definitive, even his mistakes having acquired an aura.[16] Similarly, jazz enthusiasts would probably attribute a greater aura to the 1920 recordings of Louis Armstrong than to a repertory group producing exact recreations of the music for a live audience today.

Although few Americans perceive jazz as art with an aura, Afro-American music did not develop in Storyville alone. African religion and black American Christianity also made jazz possible, and the music has as legitimate a claim to the sacral as, say, a symphony by Haydn. Benjamin's concept of the aura, however, rests on the psychological processes in the consumer of a work of art, and until recently mainstream American audiences have always perceived jazz as something completely outside the pantheon of serious art. Attempts to make a lady out of jazz have historically involved substituting some other female for the woman of dubious virtue even if figures such as Duke Ellington and John Lewis have occasionally succeeded in bringing some dignity of concert art to the real thing.

Because few would attribute to jazz an aura as understood in Benjamin's sense, the music cannot make the same statements as the historical avant-garde. In American music, the closest equivalent to Duchamp's fountain may be John Cage's *4'33"* of 1954. By exposing an unsuspecting concert audience to several minutes of a pianist sitting in silence before his instrument, Cage accomplished many of the same goals as Duchamp with his Ready-Mades. But if a jazz pianist were to rest silently for several minutes during a performance, few people would notice because the act would most likely take place in a club where audiences are often as interested in talking and drinking as they are in listening, and where some amount of unconventional behavior is expected. A certain kind of aura may exist in cabarets and jazz clubs, but hardly the sacral awe generated by a concert hall. And even in a concert hall, jazz artists appear more concerned with acquiring than with flaunting an aura.

Artists of the historical avant garde and the free jazz artists of the 1960s encountered radically different audiences. Prior to the 1920s, the Edwardian gentleman in England, the burgher in Germany, and the bourgeois in France were likely to embrace beliefs about art, beauty, and value that could be precisely and proudly articulated. The avant-gardistes of this period could find clearly

97

defined targets for their assaults. But as Ronald Radano has convincingly argued, much of the jazz community obligingly tolerated free jazz during the first half of the 1960s; the subsequent hostility toward the music came largely in response to rhetorical assaults, often on the question of race, by free jazz artists upon their critics.[17] Outside the jazz community, anyone who would have been offended by this music had already been alienated by two decades of bop eccentricities: for their natural audiences in their respective eras, the new music of the 1940s was more *epatante* than the "avant-garde jazz" of the 1960s. America's Mrs. Grundys and media vigilantes had been outraged by jazz as early as the beginning of the century, but since the 1950s they have been much more concerned with rock and roll, that inexhaustible source of menace whether it be juvenile delinquency, sexual promiscuity, drug addiction, satanism, or sexism. The esoteric sounds of jazz can provide little competition for the ubiquitous excesses of rock.

Just as unsympathetic audiences can avoid jazz altogether, those who do seek out the music have learned to tolerate and even expect a few eccentricities. Many hipsters who heard Ornette Coleman at his first New York appearance in 1959 at the Five Spot came prepared to experience a fashionable media event as much as the music.[18] Since the 1970s, the Art Ensemble of Chicago has regularly subjected audiences to Dada-like stage practices, but listeners who may not enjoy these interludes usually wait patiently for the moments when the musicians put down their "little instruments," pick up their horns, and begin their seamless evocations of black musical history. Attempts at offending the audience, no matter how flamboyant, now constitute one accepted performance practice of postmodern art.

The principal aim of the historical avant-garde was to distance itself from its audience, to attack so thoroughly its preconceptions that art and society would never be the same. The goal of the American jazz musician, however, has almost always been acceptance, even if that goal includes, as it has for the boppers and numerous artists since, an ironic stance toward that acceptance. Unlike the Dadaists, who rejected virtually all traditions of Western art, jazz musicians belong to a tradition of which Ornette Coleman and Cecil Taylor are just as much a part as Louis Armstrong and Duke Ellington. Because jazz artists are part of a tradition and are to a large extent defined by it, they cannot regularly make statements comparable to Dadaist outbursts without ceasing to be jazz musicians or, more important, employed jazz musicians.

Nevertheless, there are certain gestural affinities between the historical avant-garde and jazz, especially bebop. To make this argument, I must dwell for a few pages on the interpretations of Dada and the historical avant-garde. Marxist critics, who characterize bourgeois art as a means of perpetuating false values, have observed that avant-garde art questions the entire process by which art is institutionalized. Frequently armed with manifestoes, vanguard artists teach their public to reject bourgeois claims for art's inevitability or universality. Once the masses have made this intellectual leap, it is argued, they may then discover that they need not live with every aspect of their political and economic systems.

In an original and provocative book on avant-garde art, the German critic Peter Bürger has attributed great political importance to Dada and other elements of the historical avant-garde. Writing in the tradition of the Frankfurt School of cultural criticism, Bürger suggests that these movements have laid bare a historical process that began in the Renaissance and went undetected until the 1910s. In chart 1, he traces (p. 48) the role of European art, particularly its relationship to what he calls "the praxis of life," in terms of three categories: the purpose or function of art, its production, and its reception.

Chart 1. Art and the Praxis of Life

	Sacral art	*Courtly art*	*Bourgeois art*
Purpose or function	cult object	representa-tional object	portrayal of bourgeois self-understanding
Production	collective craft	individual	individual
Reception	collective (sacral)	collective (sociable)	individual

The sacral art of the Middle Ages functioned as a cult object, entirely integrated into religion. Art was produced collectively as a craft and experienced collectively as an essential part of that religion. Courtly art (Bürger offers the court of Louis XIV as an example) functioned as a means of glorifying royalty and its society, and although free from sacral associations, its representations of the court were just as thoroughly integrated into practical life as had been the cult paintings of medieval art. Once liberated from the sacral, the court artist produced as an individual and became aware of the uniqueness of his activity even though the reception of his works remained collective. In bourgeois society the artist continues to create as an individual, but his works are now consumed or received almost exclusively by solitary individuals. Most important, as bourgeois art begins to provide its class with self-understanding (primarily through Realist fiction and painting), works of art begin to drift away from everyday practicality. Bürger identifies the "aestheticism" of *l'art pour l'art* movements as the final severing of art's ties with practical life. When Realism, which attempts to hide the means of its artifice, is superseded by an art that stresses its own workings, the institution of art becomes essentially functionless (pp. 47–48).

The "autonomous art" of aestheticism, which is about art itself, exists entirely apart from the "means-ends rationality" of bourgeois daily life (Bürger, 49). As a result it has no social consequences and no hope of changing practical life, from which it has withdrawn. Aestheticism, however, created the conditions for the rise of avant-garde movements, such as Dada, that seek to reintegrate art into everyday reality. When Duchamp sends a Ready-Made to a museum, he attacks the distribution apparatus of art as well as the prevailing attitudes that determine how art is received; furthermore, he undermines the entire bourgeois system that gives art its autonomous status (Bürger, 22).

Bürger has special criticisms for the paragraph in Benjamin's "The Work of Art in the Age of Mechanical Reproduction" concerning the Dadaists' efforts to rid their works of an aura (quoted above). Benjamin suggested that changes in the techniques of reproduction destroy aura and hence the entire character of bourgeois art. While Benjamin credits Dada only with anticipating these technological changes, Bürger argues that the intentions of the Dadaists played a much greater historical role than any changes that followed naturally from technological innovation. Dada's use of "buttons and tickets" and "word salad" (Benjamin, 237) functions as what Bürger calls "reality fragments" that destroy not only aura but also the illusion of art's autonomy. For Bürger, collage is essential to avant-garde art because it destroys the traditional "organic" unity of a work of art. Dada marks a decisive break with the organic or classical art that seeks to express a living totally, as if works of art develop as naturally as the living forms they portray. While the classicist sees each element in a work of art as subordinate to an organic whole, the avant-gardiste exposes each fragment as simply another piece of material (Bürger, 70).

As Bürger points out (p. 80), however, the historical avant-garde must ultimately be judged a failure. The avant-garde artist, who does not give a conventional sense of "meaning" to his works and who refuses to endow his art with an impression of totality, makes the reception of these works highly problematic. This refusal to provide meaning is experienced as shock by the recipient. And this is the intention of the avant-garde artist, who hopes that such withdrawal of meaning will direct the reader's attention to the fact that the conduct of one's life is questionable and that it is necessary to change it. Because shock is a unique experience and cannot be repeated, the avant-gardiste quickly loses his political edge and is assimilated into the aestheticist mainstream. Bürger finds a contradiction between, on the one hand, the avant-garde's desire to destroy the autonomy of art, and on the other, its simultaneous desire to criticize practical life, a project that can only succeed when art is autonomous. After a Duchamp Ready-Made has lost its novelty, it becomes another document in the history of art, again separate from practical life. "If an artist today signs a stove pipe and exhibits it, that artist certainly does not denounce the art market but adapts to it" (Bürger, 52). In spite of this negative assessment, Bürger credits the avant-garde with one positive achievement: it is now impossible, he argues, for any post-avant-garde art to make a legitimate case for its validity, either permanent or temporary. By laying bare the extrinsic processes by which art acquires an aura or a place in a museum, Dada shows that no type of art can be more advanced or universal than another.

Earlier I said that jazz has sacral antecedents that are at least as strong as a Haydn symphony's even if they are insufficient to win an aura for the music in dominant culture. Bürger's system shows why jazz has these sacral antecedents. As recently as the late nineteenth century, Afro-American music was still in a sacral phase, produced and received collectively, often functioning as part of worship. The music quickly moved into a bourgeois phase, picking up influences from nonsacral sources such as military marches, polka bands, and vaudeville. Although self-consciously individual artists were soon making records for solitary consumers, blues and jazz have never completely achieved the kind of autonomy from practical life that is associated with, say, the novel. Even though bourgeois consumers listening to Billie Holiday may experience her performance as "a reflection of their self-understanding" (they too can have a broken heart), Afro-American music has always played a greater role in black life as opposed to white secular life. For this reason, the jazz artist does not have quite the same mission of reintegrating art into life praxis that Bürger attributes to the Dadaist.

Although he makes no mention of the music, Bürger's work offers a means for assessing avant-garde gestures by jazz artists. Jazz musicians have never been in a position to shake the foundations of institutionalized Western art along the lines that Bürger claims for the historical avant-gardistes. Rather than seeking to strip away a nonexistent aura from their own traditions, jazz artists strive to gain legitimacy for themselves and their music. Instead of diluting their music for a popular audience, jazz artists can find this legitimacy either by inflating jazz to the level of Western art music (Ellington, the Modern Jazz Quartet, "Third Stream" music, Anthony Davis's X) or, more important, by unmasking the music that bourgeois America privileges over jazz. Because this kind of unmasking can be dangerous and because jazz artists know they will probably never achieve real acceptance on their own terms, they frequently affect a "hip" or "cool" attitude, a manner that has become for many observers—both pro and con—as important as the music. In the bop era, this sense of ironic detachment, what James Lincoln Collier calls "silent knowingness,"[19] produced gestures that recall much of what Bürger attributes to Dada and the historical avant-garde.

Bop quotation—corresponding closely to Bürger's concept of collage—may provide the best example of how jazz artists have used the limited means at their disposal to question their culture's institutionalization of art. In the 1920s, Duke Ellington orchestrated a few bars of Chopin's "Marche Funebre" at the end of "Black and Tan Fantasy," and Freddie Jenkins quoted the most memorable lines of Rossini's "William Tell Overture" while soloing on Ellington's 1932 recording of "In the Shade of the Old Apple Tree." Although there is a playfulness to this kind of quotation, it is not unlike similar gestures by "European" composers such as Ives, Mahler, and Liszt. By skillfully integrating homages to other composers into the structure of their music, these composers can still be considered classicists who regard the work of art as an organic whole from which no part can be removed without destroying or maiming the totality. Even Ives, with his collages of sounds and melodies, created organic works of art: each sound in *The Fourth of July*, for example, fits into the total representation of how a participant might experience the holiday festivities.[20] By contrast, the jazz quoter who inserts a few bars of a middle-brow classic in the midst of an inapposite improvisation breaks the illusion of organic art, for both his own music and the composer he is citing.

In addition to the quotation of familiar melody, an avant-garde gesture may create the effect of collage by introducing seemingly nonmusical material into a solo. Functioning as another kind of Dadaist "reality fragment," this performance practice undermines art with an aura, subverts traditional notions of artistic autonomy and organicism, and invites portions of the audience to reconsider their relationship to their culture. These gestures can also connote what Calinescu finds most typical of avant-garde art: "intellectual playfulness, iconoclasm, a cult of unseriousness" (p. 125). Significantly, these practices began or became entrenched during the bop era. The bluesy imitation of the human voice was a regular practice for Charlie Parker, anticipating what Francis Davis, in an elegantly turned phrase, has referred to as the "keening vox-humana quality" of Ornette Coleman's intonation.[21] In 1960, Charles Mingus and Eric Dolphy recorded a duet in which they evoked the speech patterns of a real, apparently rather acerbic, human conversation.[22] Dolphy created an equally avant-garde collage effect when he made bird noises with his flute and duck noises with his bass clarinet.[23] Much of this can be traced back to effects developed by earlier jazz artists; for example, King Oliver played his trumpet into a water glass or a plumber's helper. There was a certain amount of nose-thumbing in these earlier gestures, but they were more like the ribald stories —with which performers such as Armstrong and Jelly Roll Morton delighted their audiences—than the dialogues with bourgeois culture undertaken by artists such as Dolphy. The boppers and their descendants were, after all, playing jazz as more an art music, but an art music that questioned the audience's aesthetic attitudes at the same time that it allowed for explorations of an instrument's sonoric possibilities.

As for "Country Gardens," the tune is an irresistible vehicle for jazz improvisation, even if the artist who quotes it has no conscious "signifying" intentions. The melody's infectious simplicity falls easily under the fingers of the jazz improviser, and its most frequently quoted phrase moves from tonic to dominant and then back to tonic, a cadence found at the endings of many melodies that the boppers were fond of transforming. Similarly, Charlie Parker would begin a phrase by quoting the opening bars of Alphonse Picou's clarinet solo on "High Society," a motif that can be used wherever a chorus begins on two measures of the tonic.[24] But the artists of Parker's generation may also have found that "Country Gardens," when performed along with the other gestures of a jazz performance, signifies on fatuous, bourgeois art music by emphasizing the passion and complexity of the new Afro-American art music. Playing together on a 1950 recording, Parker, Gillespie, and Monk used "Country Gardens" to make a richly avant-garde gesture.[25] At the conclusion of "My Melancholy Baby," Parker suddenly stops in the middle of a phrase, both submitting the old chestnut to parody and creating a mock "mistake," another type of limited gesture with an avant-garde character.[26] Then Parker and Gillespie together toss off a few measures of "Country Gardens," concluding with a baroque trill as if to place a powdered wig inelegantly on the head of Grainger and the tradition he represents.[27]

A substantial repertoire of light classical melodies taken from compositions such as *Carmen, The Peer Gynt Suite, The Grand Canyon Suite*, "Humoresque," "The March of the Wooden Soldiers," "The Kerry Dance," and "The Glow Worm"[28] has provided jazz improvisers with the same qualities as "Country Gardens." But the most prolific quoters seldom limit themselves to this body of music: Dexter Gordon has performed solos that are little more than perversely truncated medleys of popular songs with brief interludes of more conventionally improvised material. I do not wish to suggest, however, that an artist such as Charlie Parker could not have been of two minds about his relationship to the music of white and/or "high" culture, or that he was not capable of compartmentalizing his listeners. While club audiences might have appreciated his ironic allusions to Grainger, Grieg, Rossini, or Bizet, Parker seems to have been quite sincere in his efforts to expand his audience (and his own resources as a musician) by performing with a lachrymose string orchestra. There is also no doubt that he genuinely admired Honegger, Stravinsky, Hindemith, and Varese, but these are not the composers he felt obliged to quote.[29] And although Parker did give his compositions titles such as "Passport" and "Visa" when the State Department was about to revoke Paul Robeson's passport in 1949, Parker's music was not overtly political in any conventional sense. It was left to a more radical artist like Charles Mingus to take the art of ironic quotation a step farther and quote "God Bless America" in a 1951 club date with Parker.[30]

Parker also expresses a certain amount of ambivalence when he quotes from Alphonse Picou or Armstrong's opening cadenza on "West End Blues."[31] Serge Chaloff makes an even more complex gesture when, in an extremely *lento* version of a song ("Body and Soul") most closely associated with Coleman Hawkins, he quotes from Lester Young's up-tempo solo on Count Basie's "Jive at Five."[32] These quotations of jazz within a jazz performance—and in the case of Chaloff, the quotation of a black artist by a white artist at the expense of another black artist—can be understood as a more advanced form of signifying. Whether the intent is Dadaist, these intertextual references address the aura that the monumental recordings of the quoted giant have acquired in the jazz community. (Both Armstrong's "West End Blues" and Hawkins's "Body and Soul" are included in *The Smithsonian Collection of Classic Jazz,* the nearest equivalent to a "canon" of jazz recordings.) The quoters' gestures reveal the ambivalent relationship that each generation of jazz musicians bears to the preceding ones. Any understanding of signifying in jazz must allow for the possibility that musicians signify on those they respect as well as on those they do not.[33]

Bürger has said that no disruption of art practice can sustain its avant-garde character for long. By the late 1950s, collage effects like the quotation of light classics had become normalized gestures in jazz improvisation, increasingly devoid of the quiet irony essential to the boppers' cultural stance. As jazz and black Americans moved toward greater acceptance, the avant-garde practices of the 1940s lost their impact. Subsequent developments in jazz history are consistent with a *new* avant-garde that Calinescu identifies in Europe and America after World War II (p. 144). Among its ranks he lists the Italian *Gruppo 63,* the French novelists of the "nouveauroman," the Parisian *Tel Quel* group, the concrete poets, anarchist members of the Beat movement, Pop artists, the Living Theatre, and John Cage. We might add action painting, happenings, and performance art as well as certain branches of the jazz community. Even popular music has found room for conceptualist poseurs such as David Byrne and Laurie Anderson, whose roots are in this tradition. This new avant-garde has undertaken a theoretical appropriation of the historical avant-garde at the same time that "both the rhetoric of destruction and that of novelty have lost their heroic appeal" (Calinescu, 146–47). The agonistic, anarchist intentions of Dada, Surrealism, and Futurism have become institutionalized, and the anti-aestheticism of the old avant-garde has become one of many available aesthetics in the cultural marketplace. In the words of Jean-Francois Lyotard, "eclecticism is the degree zero of contemporary general culture."[34]

But as Bürger and many others have observed, the old avant-garde had the fortuitous effect of permanently eroding the distinction between high and low art. This development has made possible the growing recognition in the postmodern era of achievements by artists in jazz and other previously suspect art forms. Critics now find art coexisting comfortably with kitsch in the currents of mass culture. Andreas Huyssen, for example, singles out the films of Rainer Werner Fassbinder as typical of what happened in the 1970s when "artists increasingly drew on popular or mass cultural forms and genres, overlaying them with modernist and/or avant-gardist strategies."[35] In jazz, Lester Bowie's recent deconstructions of rhythm-and-blues ballads from the 1950s represent a comparable "overlaying" of previously incompatible forms.[36] Bowie alludes to the revised prestige of jazz by inverting the implicit hierarchy that in Parker's day provoked the altoist to signify on white classics from "below"; in the whimsical order of Bowie's musical universe, jazz can now signify on pop music from "above."

If a handful of gestures initiated primarily by beboppers is as close as jazz comes to the old avant-garde, the pluralism of some recent jazz is most consistent with the new postmodern avant-garde. At its best, this pluralism is informed but not pedantic, serious but not academic, energetic but not chaotic, playful but not mocking. David Murray, perhaps the most widely celebrated of a new generation of "neoclassicists," can invoke equal portions of Sidney Bechet, Duke Ellington, Charles Mingus, and Albert Ayler in a single performance, even in a single phrase. When bop, the last jazz to be rooted primarily in jazz traditions, had played itself out in its various manifestations in the 1940s and 1950s, the music began its perhaps inevitable march toward pluralism with Taylor and Coleman, even as their music alienated large portions of the jazz audience. Taylor's grounding in European art music and Coleman's harmolodic manifestoes are consistent with this intellectualist neo-avant-garde. In fact, the term "avant-garde" was waiting to be applied to them after it had been widely used in connection with a New York–based avant-garde revival in the 1950s that included Jackson Pollock, John Cage, and Allen Ginsberg. Since the advent of Taylor and Coleman, musicians such as Murray, Bowie, Henry Threadgill, Craig Harris, and Muhal Richard Abrams have earned critical attention by learning the history of the music and synthesizing many of its elements. A new music now exists that has assimilated nihilistic aspects of the old avant-garde, not as a demand for self-destruction but, perhaps paradoxically, as an affirmation of the past. Furthermore, this music has moved beyond the crisis that faced a self-conscious innovator like Miles Davis who saw only three avenues left open to him in the late 1960s: a calcification of his earlier styles, an abandonment of his audience with a move into free jazz, and a defection to the popular mainstream.[37] The new music does not have and never will have the large audience that Davis drew when he first embraced fusion, but it does show other solutions to Davis's dilemma.

For better or worse, today's jazz artists create in a climate of postmodern live-and-let-live, and, as a result, they can move away from the agonistic and political postures that made the first free jazz artists controversial and thus likely to be labeled "avant-garde," a term that has always had pejorative as well as positive connotations. In spite of the occasional notoriety of a figure such as Allen Bloom, the same bourgeoisie that made the old avant-garde possible is for all practical purposes dead. Today, the best definition of avant-gardism in jazz is pluralism rather than anti-bourgeois ferocity. As for the quoters, their reservoir of quotable material is now as diverse as their attitudes toward an America that still cannot make up its mind about jazz: in spite of some recent easing of prejudices against the music, it still possesses too little of an aura to be fully institutionalized along with "classical" music and too much of an aura to be widely embraced as "popular" music.

Notes

1. James Moody, "Body and Soul," rec. Oct. 12, 1949 (Prestige LP110).
2. Parker does this repeatedly on the radio broadcasts anthologized on *Bird at the Roost: The Savoy Years*, Vols. 1, 2, and 3 (Savoy SJL 2259, 2260 and 1173).

3. Barry Kernfeld, "Two Coltranes," *Annual Review of Jazz Studies* 2 (1983): 7–66. In building his convincing theory of jazz improvisation, Kernfeld has appropriated the work of musicologist Leo Treitler, who cites theorists of oral poetry (Milman Parry, Alfred Lord, Ruth Finnegan, etc.) in his work on the transmission of medieval music.

4. Geneva Smitherman has defined "signifying" as Afro-American argot for "the verbal art of insult in which a speaker humorously puts down, talks about, needles—that is, signifies on—the listener." See her *Talking and Testifying* (Boston: Houghton Mifflin, 1975), 118. Henry Louis Gates has made this practice—which he calls "Signifyin(g)" in order to distinguish it from the standard English sense of the word—the central concept in his *The Signifying Monkey: A Theory of Afro-American Literary Criticism* (New York: Oxford University Press, 1986). Although his book dwells only briefly on jazz, Gates is correct in his assertion, "There are so many examples of Signifyin(g) in jazz that one could write a formal history of its development on this basis alone" (63).

5. Peter Bürger, *Theory of the Avant-Garde*, trans. Michael Shaw. Theory and History of Literature 4 (Minneapolis: University of Minneseota Press, 1984), 72. A number of critics have addressed the question of quotation and collage in music. A good discussion of the subject is in Ulrich Weisstein's "Collage, Montage, and Related Terms: Their Literal and Figurative Use in and Application to Techniques and Forms in Various Arts," *Comparative Literature Studies* 15 (1978): 124–39. Also see Nelson Goodman, "On Some Questions Concerning Quotation," *Monist* 58 (1974): 294–306; V. A. Howard, "On Musical Quotation," *Monist* 58 (1974): 307–18; and Wendy Steiner, ed., *The Sign in Music and Literature* (Austin: University of Texas Press, 1981).

6. Louis Armstrong, "Ain't Misbehavin,'" rec. July 19, 1929, *V.S.O.P.* 5 (French CBS 88003).

7. James Lincoln Collier, *Louis Armstrong: An American Genius* (New York: Oxford University Press, 1983), 166–67, 317–19. Also see William Howland Kenney III's account in this volume of "the carefully orchestrated versions of himself" that Armstrong slipped past editors and ghostwriters in his autobiographical statements.

8. While this assertion is difficult to document, see the suggestive concluding pages of Lewis Porter's book in which he portrays Young as deeply involved with the substance of his art: "Pres Returns," *Lester Young* (Boston: Twayne, 1985), 99–105. By singling out artists such as Young, Armstrong, and Parker throughout this essay, I do not intend to establish a "great man" theory of jazz history. Rather, I have chosen their works to typify the major crises in the development of the music. Most important, these artists have attracted the greatest attention of record collectors, and thus a wide selection of their music—including radio broadcasts and informal jam sessions—is available on disc. I would like to extend this aside

in order to agree with several readers who have observed that two structuring absences in my argument are Art Tatum and Thelonius Monk. Tatum's encyclopedic quoting was surely an inspiration for Charlie Parker and deserves an entire study of its own. Monk's place in any definitive study of bebop performance practice would be marked by the pianist's studied *refusal* to quote in the collage style favored by boppers.

9. Gary Giddins, *Celebrating Bird: The Triumph of Charlie Parker* (New York: William Morrow, 1987), 77.

10. See especially Norman Mailer, *The White Negro* (San Francisco: City Lights, 1959).

11. Matei Calinescu, *Five Faces of Modernity: Modernism, Avant-Garde, Decadence, Kitsch, Postmodernism* (Durham: Duke University Press, 1987), 119.

12. Tristan Tzara, *Seven Dada Manifestoes and Lampisteries*, trans. Barbara Wright (London: John Calder, 1977), 39.

13. For a good discussion of these predominantly French attitudes toward jazz, see Ted Gioia, "Jazz and the Primitivist Myth," in *The Imperfect Art* (New York: Oxford University Press, 1988), 19–49.

14. Roger Shattuck, *The Banquet Years: The Origins of the Avant Garde in France, 1885 to World War I*, rev. ed. (New York: Random House, 1968), 153–58.

15. "The Work of Art in the Age of Mechanical Reproduction," in *Illuminations*, trans. Harry Zohn (New York: Schocken Books, 1969), 217–51.

16. The aura attached to the historical monuments of European concert music is a distinctively twentieth-century phenomenon. In previous eras, many composers were author-performers of their own work, and improvisation was an accepted part of virtuoso performance practice. The idea that culturally enshrined works of composers such as Bach and Mozart ought to be played on original instruments with exact recreation of their original sound has become commonplace only in the last few decades.

17. Ronald M. Radano, "The Jazz Avant-Garde and the Jazz Community: Action and Reaction," *Annual Review of Jazz Studies* 3 (1985): 73–76.

18. See Irving Louis Horowitz, "On Seeing and Hearing Music: Nine Propositions in Search of Explanation," *Annual Review of Jazz Studies* 1 (1982): 72–78.

19. *The Making of Jazz* (New York: Dell, 1978), p. 360.

20. For a somewhat different approach to the subject, see Christopher Ballantine, "Charles Ives and the Meaning of Quotation in Music," *Music and its Social Meanings* (New York: Gordon and Breach, 1984), 72–91. A convincing argument for placing Ives more securely in European (and "organic") musical traditions can be found in Robert P. Morgan, "Ives and Mahler: Mutual Responses at the End of an Era," *Nineteenth Century Music* 2 (1978): 72–81.

21. *In the Moment: Jazz in the 1980s* (New York: Oxford University Press, 1986), 137.

22. Charles Mingus, "What Love," rec. Oct. 20, 1960, *The Complete Candid Recordings of Charles Mingus* (Mosaic MR4- 111).

23. On, respectively, "Gazzeloni," rec. Feb. 25, 1964, *Out to Lunch* (Blue Note BST 84163), and the ending of the previously cited "What Love."

24. Parker quotes Picou on "Warming Up a Riff," rec. Nov. 26, 1945, *The Complete Savoy Studio Sessions* (Savoy 5500). Parker is quoting more in the tradition of Lester Young at this stage, also citing "Shortenin' Bread," "The Campbells Are Coming," and "Cocktails for Two" in his solo. Significantly, Parker did not know he was being recorded when he played "Warming Up a Riff" in the studio. Throughout most of the 1940s, Parker was more circumspect about quoting when he knew that his performances were being preserved for posterity.

25. Charlie Parker, "My Melancholy Baby," rec. June 6, 1950, *The Verve Years (1948–50)* (Verve VE-2-2501.) Early in his solo on "Relaxin' with Lee" at the same recording session, Parker flamboyantly quotes a comparable piece of middle-brow white music, the Habanera from Bizet's *Carmen*.

26. Miles Davis is perhaps the best-known jazz musician whose "mistakes" have become an accepted part of his artistry, for example, his famous fluff on "My Funny Valentine," rec. Feb. 12, 1964, *My Funny Valentine* (Columbia PC 9106). The gesture shows contempt for Western art music with its smooth, "organic" surfaces, its technical precision, and its highly stylized set of emotional codes. This aestheticization of error and chance is also consistent with the aleatoric experiments of "serious" vanguard composers such as John Cage and Pierre Boulez.

27. Today, "Country Gardens" is still associated with the values of an overly cultivated social class. As of August 1989, boxer Marvin Hagler appears in a deodorant commercial on television in which he self-consciously mimics an affluent English gentleman on his carefully manicured estate while "Country Gardens" plays in the background. Just as the song provided black jazz artists with an ironic contrast to their own music, in the commercial, "Country Gardens" offers an amusing foil for the assumed milieu of a black boxer. A similar commercial for the same deodorant features white athlete Brian Bosworth but does not have "Country Gardens" as a musical backdrop.

28. Although it quickly entered the more popular repertoire, "Glow Worm" was written by the German composer Paul Lincke (1866–1946) and was first performed in 1902 in his operetta *Lysistrata*. The introductory bars of "Glow Worm" are frequently quoted by bop improvisers, e.g., Dizzy Gillespie with the Metronome All-Stars, "Overtime," rec. Jan. 3, 1949, *Dizzy Gillespie, Vols. 1 and 2* (RCA PM 42 408), and Charlie Parker with a Canadian group on "Don't Blame Me," rec. Feb. 5, 1953, *Bird on the Road* (Jazz Showcase 5003).

29. In personal correspondence, James Patrick has suggested that Parker quotes from Stravinsky's *Firebird* on "Cool Blues," rec. 1949, *Charlie Parker* (Queen Disc 002). The New York disc jockey and record producer Phil Schaap has said that Parker quotes from *Le Sacre du printemps* at the very beginning of his solo on "Repetition," rec. Autumn 1948, *The Verve Years (1948–50)* (Verve VE2-2501). If one listens only to the alto solo, it does sound as if Parker is referencing Stravinsky, but it is just as likely that Parker is repeating a motif from Neal Hefti's arrangement for strings that precedes his solo by a few bars. Schaap points out that this particular recording marked the first occasion in which Parker played in Carnegie Hall. It would be especially poignant for Parker to pay homage to someone like Stravinsky as he recorded his first notes in a locale with the aura of Carnegie. Still, it could be argued just as strongly that Neal Hefti is quoting *Le Sacre* and that Parker is quoting Hefti, perhaps ironically.

30. On Charlie Parker, "I'll Remember April," rec. April 12, 1951, *The Happy Bird* (Charlie Parker PLP404).

31. Charlie Parker, "Visa," rec. Feb. 18, 1950, *Charlie Parker* (Prestige 24009); Parker quoted from "West End Blues" less explicitly on "Cheryl," rec. Dec. 24, 1949, *Bird's Perch* (Parktec 4627).

32. Serge Chaloff, "Body and Soul," rec. Apr. 4, 1955, *Boston Blow-Up* (Capitol T6510).

33. Although I am not convinced that Jelly Roll Morton necessarily held Scott Joplin in the highest regard, in *The Signifying Monkey*, Gates argues that Morton's "Signifyin(g)" on Joplin's "Maple Leaf Rag" in his 1938 Library of Congress recording is "a gesture of admiration and respect" (63).

34. *The Postmodern Condition: A Report on Knowledge*, trans. Geoff Bennington and Brian Massumi. Theory and History of Literature 10 (Minneapolis: University of Minnesota Press, 1984), 76.

35. Andreas Huyssen, "Mapping the Postmodern," *New German Critique*, no. 33 (Fall 1984): 27; rpt. in Huyssen's *After the Great Divide* (Bloomington: Indiana University Press, 1986).

36. Hear Bowie's "The Great Pretender," rec. June 1981, *The Great Pretender* (ECM 1209), and "I Only Have Eyes for You," rec. Feb. 1985, *I Only Have Eyes for You* (ECM 1296).

37. For a good discussion of Davis's thinking during the late 1960s, see Ian Carr, *Miles Davis* (New York: William Morrow, 1982), 148–64.

"JAZZ ISN'T JUST ME": JAZZ AUTOBIOGRAPHIES as PERFORMANCE PERSONAS

Kathy Ogren

Jazz was a controversial new music in the 1920s that prompted a spirited debate throughout American society. Beginning with the earliest articles either favoring or attacking jazz, the history of the music has been characterized by a combination of verifiable information, legends, and apocryphal stories.

Autobiographies, like oral histories, are useful first-hand sources of information on early jazz. Like all autobiographies, jazz artists' first-person stories are also suspect as definitive versions of historical events because they are highly subjective accounts. But researchers should not reject the autobiography because of its lack of corroborative evidence, its tendency toward self-aggrandizement on the part of the narrator, or the possibility of distortions created by editors. Jazz autobiographies are textual performances in which musicians, sometimes in concert with their amanuensis, create personas equally as fascinating as those developed musically. Historians need to recognize the possibilities—not merely the limitations—of self-fashioned personas.

Jazz autobiographies are useful not only as records of an individual life, but as examples of a rich expressive tradition. When these texts are studied collectively they reveal several formulaic qualities; in some cases, the stories have been repeated so frequently they have essentially become jazz folklore. Autobiographies by African-American jazz musicians differ significantly from other autobiographical collections, however, because these texts communicate recurring themes about the origins of jazz and its development as an art and entertainment form that relied on participatory exchanges between musicians and their audiences. The musical inspiration for jazz autobiographies is reinforced by influences from the black oral tradition, especially verbal strategies expressed through storytelling, bragging, and humor.

New Orleans reed player Sidney Bechet provided an eloquent example of the reciprocal relationships between individual performers and African-American storytelling when he opened his autobiography, *Treat It Gentle* (1960), with this meditation:

> My story goes a long way back. It goes further back than I had anything to do with. My music is like that . . . I got it from something inherited, just like the stories my father gave down to me. And those stories are all I know about some of the things bringing me to where I am. And all my life I've been trying to explain about something, something I understand— the part of me that was there before I was. It was there waiting to be me. It was there waiting to be the music. It's that part I've been trying to explain to myself all my life.[1]

Bechet depicts his autobiography as a structure "waiting" to be filled with his individual improvisation—much like the creative processes central to the African-American music he had mastered.

Bechet's autobiographical persona is comparable to those presented by other early jazzmen, in particular, Louis Armstrong's *Satchmo: My Life in New Orleans* (1954) and Alan Lomax's biography of Jelly Roll Morton, *Mister Jelly Roll: The Fortunes of Jelly Roll Morton, New Orleans Creole and "Inventor" of Jazz* (1986). These musicians portray a self and a music created antiphonally—that is, out of a call and response between the musician and his audience, family, musical heritage, other musicians, and, in some cases, an editor or amanuensis.

One profitable method for analyzing jazz autobiographies is to consider their similar, even repetitive, characteristics as a basic framework within which individually distinctive personas are created. By outlining several features common to autobiographies of early jazzmen and then looking at three different textual strategies used to create authority within that tradition, one can see the participatory performance dynamics of jazz music translated into the musicians' persona. Amanuenses served a crucial role in many cases by acting as directors of or players in the autobiographical occasion.[2]

All the jazzmen under discussion contributed to a larger pattern of oral performances characteristic of early jazzmen. Their autobiographical personas, as well as their music, have been quite important to our understanding of early jazz. These autobiographies should not be rejected for any lack of accuracy but rather applauded as impressive performances.

Some similarities among the five autobiographical personas are predictable because these men performed during the first era of jazz. Armstrong, Bechet, and Danny Barker are strongly associated with early heterophonic ensemble style jazz, especially as it first developed in New Orleans. Willie "the Lion" Smith and Morton played ragtime, stride, and jazz piano, which are more clearly expressions of individual performance styles. But these pianists also acknowledged the influence of audience response on their music, making participatory performance traditions a central feature of each musical career depicted in these texts.

Similarly, all these autobiographies use travel as a main theme, and certain characteristics of musicians' experiences ensure that the metaphor carries tremendous force in these narratives. For example, the central idea linking much of Bechet's story is that of the road: "'The music, its that road. . . . You stop by the way and you can't ever be sure what you're going to find waiting. But the music itself—the road itself—there's no stopping that. . . . You have to trust that. There's no one ever came back who can't tell you that.'"[3] Although Bechet's use of the journey motif may seem a mere convention of autobiographical writing, it is also true that a musician's life is literally organized around migratory work patterns; their creative growth, paralleled in the dissemination of jazz itself, is well illustrated through geographic shifts. In jazz, and especially in blues, the road is recognized as a central symbol of black social history generally.[4]

One can clearly see how the geographical basis for formulaic aspects of these stories developed by looking at how Louis Armstrong, Sidney Bechet, Jelly Roll Morton, and Danny Barker all present the beginnings of their lives in New Orleans. When these musicians described their origins, urban geography and family ties often merged in the portraits drawn. All of them began performing at an early age, often as a result of family influences or connections.

Bechet started playing by imitating his brother Leonard. Barker, raised in the French Quarter, was a grandson of the famous bandleader Isidore Barbarin. Ferdinand La Menthe, better known as Jelly Roll Morton, came from a family that tolerated music only if it corresponded to the style of the French opera house. Armstrong was raised in and around a tough section of New Orleans near black Storyville. His first musical experience was with a quartet of other young children, with whom he hustled tunes on the street. This, too, was not unusual for aspiring jazz musicians. Barker, for example, performed in a "spasm" band called the Boozan Kings.[5]

In each autobiography, the significance of family and community influences on music is captured through strong evocations of place and the literal sounds of a city that the musicians credit with inspiration. Danny Barker recalled the influential sounds of his neighborhood. He described "peddlers," for example, like "the ice cream man, the snowball man, the crab man, each with a song or some noise to identify them and their wares." In addition, Barker heard "night and day people walking along singing popular jazz songs, sad mournful spirituals . . . virtuosos whistling jazz songs just like their favorite musicians played."[6]

Jelly Roll Morton dated his musical beginnings to a saloon. According to Morton, his godmother allowed a "sporting woman" to show Morton off at a local bar. A "fracas" ensued, and Morton was sent to jail with the prostitute where he supposedly chortled with glee at the music he heard. Morton did occasionally perform in a brothel, and one effect of this tale is to perpetuate the mythological importance of sporting life on early jazz. In fact, Morton received music training from a variety of sources.[7]

Although he was not born in New Orleans, Willie "the Lion" Smith's autobiography emphasizes several of the same experiences depicted by the New Orleans jazzmen. Smith identified both his vaudevillian ancestors and his mother's church music as early inspirations. Like many jazz pianists, Smith found himself torn between "proper" music and "devil's" music—the latter identified as ragtime, blues, and jazz. Urban sounds also influenced Smith, who recalled the sounds of pigs being slaughtered where his father worked as an early "rather weird but musical sound" that he heard as a child.[8]

As Smith's autobiography demonstrates, New Orleans was not

the only city where ragtime, blues, and jazz emerged. But New Orleans did offer a fertile combination of performance opportunities that made it one of the foremost environments in which musicians created jazz. The city, according to some jazz historians, was more tolerant of Afro-American slave culture than cities dominated by Anglo-Saxon values.[9] More important, New Orleans had a varied musical life, including street bands, theatre orchestras, amateur musical societies, and opera. The musical traditions and institutions of New Orleans were important not simply because musical performances were available to many residents but also because they provided employment, some private instruction, and inspiration to the earliest ragtime and jazz musicians.

In the New Orleans autobiographies of Morton, Barker, Bechet, and Armstrong, each man emphasizes the formative role provided by participatory musical traditions in the city. Each account includes a description of early performance environments that nurtured participatory jazz. For example, all the New Orleans players remember marching bands and the participation of a "second line" of dancers and performers. Jelly Roll Morton described a typical performance:

> Those parades were really tremendous things. The drums would start off, the trumpets and trombones rolling into something like *Stars and Stripes* or *The National Anthem* and everybody would strut off down the street, the bass-drum player twirling his beater in the air, the snare drummer throwing his sticks up and bouncing them off the ground, the kids jumping and hollering, the grand marshall and his aides in their expensive uniforms moving along dignified, women on top of women strutting along back of the aides and put in front of everybody —the second line, armed with sticks and bottles and baseball bats and all forms of ammunition ready to fight the foe when they reached the dividing line.[10]

Like Morton, Bechet and Barker recalled that the second line was an important way for novice musicians and members of the audience to participate in musical festivities, including in some cases, funerals. Whatever their individual ability, each man learned to test himself against the musical expectations of his elders and his audience.[11]

One main opportunity for competition with other musicians came during "bucking" and "cutting" contests, which usually took place outdoors and involved nearby audiences. These competitions between bands tested the relative skill of each group, and, as Bechet related, the winners received the acclaim of the crowd: "One band, it would come right up in front of the other and play at it, and the first band would play right back, until finally one band just had to give in. And the one that didn't give in, all the people, they'd rush up to it and give it drinks and food and holler for more, wanting more, not having enough."[12] Some of these tests were played off of the back of advertising wagons, which solicited business for evening performances in saloons, dance halls, and other nighttime venues.

Although Willie "the Lion" Smith did not grow up surrounded by these New Orleans participatory musical experiences, he explained how audiences could also affect stride pianists performing alone and inside a dance hall or saloon, rather than outside in street parades. While playing for New York clubs that catered primarily to migrants from the South, Smith learned to make the dancing tastes of recent arrivals part of his own musical style:

> These people came from around the Carolinas and Georgia sea islands. They were called Gullahs and Geechies. . . . The Gullahs would start out early in the evening dancing two-steps, waltzes, schottishes; but as the night wore on and the liquor began to work, they would start improvising their own steps and that was when they wanted us to get in the alley real lowdown.[13]

Call-and-response patterns informed the majority of performance experiences that early jazz musicians described, regardless of whether they played indoors or outdoors.

One major stage of any musician's life is his "coming of age" as a performer. In these jazz autobiographies, each man attested to his relative lack of training in sight-reading and other "formal" kinds of music education. Jelly Roll Morton studied piano at a young age, but he picked up much of his musical inspiration from listening to others. Willie "the Lion" Smith learned to play by ear because it was not, as he wrote in his autobiography, "like today when young musicians try to learn by listening to phonograph recordings."[14] Louis Armstrong received his first formal music lessons at the Jones Waifs Home in New Orleans, and he credited Bunk Johnson and Joe "King" Oliver as early influences when he began to play in adult bands.[15]

Apprenticeship periods often required a young musician to

test himself against his elders. Sidney Bechet describes how he was "discovered." While waiting for clarinetist George Baquet to come and lead his band at a family party, Bechet hid himself in a back room and played along alone. When the guests found Bechet, they were shocked at his proficiency. He was then asked to sit in for the rest of the evening—even after Baquet arrived. Bechet then received music lessons from Baquet as a result of his impressive playing, a gift that Bechet said made him feel like "the richest kid in New Orleans." Bechet went on to prove himself at a young age.[16]

Growing up in an influential New Orleans musical family gave Danny Barker early exposure to the lives of professional musicians. Bechet's quick acceptance was unusual, and most newcomers, according to Barker, found it difficult to break into more established bands. Amateur status ended when a young player joined a band or substituted for an older player. This debut was witnessed by the larger community of musicians, and, according to Bechet,

> It was rough because you were constantly watching and waiting for an opening. Musicians in New Orleans eat, sleep, and talk music, gossiping and relaying news, scandal, anything that happens. You could bet in twelve hours everybody in hearing distance would hear the news, generally amplified out of proportion good or bad. If a youngster was seen playing with a star-name band, everybody soon knew, and anything that happened on the bandstand.[17]

Musicians rose to prominence amidst competition as well as support, even those like Barker who had strong family connections. For Barker and others, it was a process that involved the response of New Orleans music lovers as well as other performers.

As the early sections of each autobiography demonstrate, these musicians describe various events and influences that contributed to their emergence as jazz performers. But they also illustrate their connections to black audiences and to each other by the ways in which they tell their stories. Armstrong, Bechet, Smith, Morton, and Barker are famous because of their musical talents, which in most cases did not require the use of lyrics. With the exception of Armstrong, these performers are primarily known as instrumentalists; yet, each autobiography reveals them as "men of words." These verbal performers are conscious of a variety of story-telling methods that help communicate their persona, and many

of their techniques are drawn from African-American oral performance traditions that also relied on the understanding and participation of audiences.[18]

Locating themselves as not only musicians but also African-
American storytellers also helps these authors establish credibility
as autobiographical speakers. This authority can be difficult to assert in any autobiography, and especially hard for performers of
music that was sometimes denigrated as a marginal creative art
by the white-dominated critical establishment in America.[19] These
men may have been particularly aware of the potentially controversial nature of jazz performance since they came of musical age
at a time when jazz was hotly debated in American society.

Sidney Bechet uses storytelling most thoroughly in his text.
He begins his genealogical explanation with a story of love, escape,
and violent death concerning his slave grandfather Omar. According to Bechet, Omar fell in love with a young slave woman named
Marie, whom Omar had seen at the legendary Congo Square
dances. Omar acquires a powerful potion, presumably from a voo-
doo practitioner, to woo Marie. When Marie's jealous white master
discovers the young lovers, he shoots and wounds Omar. Then the
master accuses Omar of raping his own daughter, rather than acknowledging his own infatuation with Marie. Omar initially escapes
into the wilds of the bayou but later returns to rescue Marie. Omar
is killed by a treacherous friend who wants the plantation owner's
reward. Eventually the plantation owner's real motivations are revealed, and Marie gives birth to Bechet's father.

As several commentators note, Bechet's epic story was most
likely apocryphal and possibly based on Louisiana folk tales.[20] But
it serves an interesting purpose in the text. Bechet choreographs
Omar's quest against the backdrop of powerful music—thus illus-
trating his contention that jazz developed from African music used
by the slaves and in particular that it communicates collective concerns. Toward the end of the autobiography, Bechet states that
"Omar started the song. Or maybe he didn't start it exactly. There
was somebody singing and playing the drums and the horns behind Omar, and there was somebody behind that. But it was Omar
began the melody of it, the new thing." Bechet's rendition of Omar's
tale places Bechet at the very beginning of the new music. It also
acknowledges the role of a community-based creative process, in
which, to borrow cultural critic Houston A. Baker's conceptual-
ization of black discursive strategies, members of maroon socie-

119

ties often conveyed cultural "soundings" by "communicating by horns."[21]

Similarly, Willie "the Lion" Smith opens his autobiography by emphasizing the origins of jazz in collective black life. "What they call jazz is just the music of people's emotions," wrote Smith. "It comes from wherever there have been colored people gathered together during the last hundred years." In particular, Smith believed, "All the different forms can be traced back to Negro church music, and the Negroes have worshipped God for centuries, whether they live in Africa, the southern United States, or in the New York City area."[22] As musicians from the first generation of jazz performance, men like Bechet and Smith simply extend their authority as musical storytellers into a broader context.

Another way in which musicians identify their individual importance, while at the same time recognizing traditions they share with other performers, is by noting their relationship to legendary performers. For example, each New Orleans player relates a story about Buddy Bolden. Bolden, a popular trumpet player during the early twentieth century, was never recorded, yet he lived on in many musicians' memories as one of the first men to play with a jazz style. Yet, as Danny Barker ironically points out, men also developed reputations as great performers precisely because they became "forgotten"—not remembered like Bolden. Barker, in an attempt to clarify who some of these might have been, describes dozens in his chapter "Feudin' and a Fussin'." Barker concludes his autobiography by describing his role as an interpreter at the New Orleans Jazz Museum, implicitly asserting his own role in that long line of great New Orleans musicians.[23]

Emphasizing one's connections to black history or great performers is just one way these authors build authority for their autobiographical persona. Several incorporate another approach in their accounts by promising to set the record straight or tell the true story of jazz. Bechet promises to tell the "real story" in his first chapter.

Willie "the Lion" Smith, rejecting New Orleans chauvinism, opens his account by declaring: "You'd think from reading the jazz books, most of them written by non-playing so-called critics, that all the jazz and all the musicians came from New Orleans. They'd have you believing that if a musician had not been born down in those swamps, down in the Delta country, he had no business trying to play jazz." Smith establishes his claim to tell a better story

about jazz than the tales told by professional historians and critics
—a process in which he tries to further legitimate his autobiographical persona.[24]

When these authors argue in print with other musicians or
with purported jazz authorities, they are doing more than simply
trying to tell the real story. These autobiographical accounts can
be seen as literary "cutting contests," in which the musician/narra-
tors display their storytelling skills. Danny Barker opens his autobiography by relating his annoyance with the way in which a major
magazine covered jazz. "I read all these *Esquire* articles," he wrote,
"and one thing that annoyed me very much was that not one musician respected as an authority in his profession . . . was on one
of the judge's panels." Barker was further irritated because these
judges were "a conglomeration of assorted leeches and self-
appointed critics. . . . Many books came on the scene together with
many falsehoods, lies and cooked up stories. I read much of this
crap and then I was told I should write some truth and explanations of many jazz subjects that were not clearly explained."[25] Like
Smith, Barker announces that he's ready to take on the so-called
experts and promises to outdo the braggarts.

When Barker describes the events that prompted his autobiography, he mentions a "lip riot" that took place between Jelly Roll
Morton and blues composer W. C. Handy. Morton was reputed to
tell stories about jazz that some considered self-serving and untrue.
Morton accused Handy of taking credit for blues tunes that had
been composed by other men, including Morton. Morton's claims
have been questioned by a number of scholars and researchers,
and even Lomax considered Morton's stories to be the stuff of legends rather than a reliable memory. But after carefully research-
ing Morton's assertions, Lawrence Gushee has concluded that
Morton's "oral autobiography, particularly when he recounts events
in which he directly participated, is quite reliable, although the
manner of telling is often exaggerated." Gushee's emphasis on the
"manner of the telling" points to the importance of the process,
not just the content of the stories told in autobiographical texts.

Morton, like the trickster in traditional African-American
folktales, may well have told his story to stir things up, not set
them straight. Exaggeration here is not a negative characteristic,
but a tactic that needs to be done well to impress the audience,
who are most likely "in" on the joke. Historian Al Rose observed
that Sidney Bechet could also use this technique: "Much of what

Sidney Bechet wrote in *Treat It Gentle* is apocryphal, to say the least. He had a way of brushing off interviewers by telling them lies so transparent as to be obvious: 'I made my first soprano sax myself in 1906, but it got stolen by Attakapas Indians when I was nine. Years later I saw it in Uncle Jake's Pawn Shop!'" "Lying" in these contexts is evidence of creativity rather than duplicity.

When one looks at Morton's account of his life and music, as preserved on the Library of Congress recordings, it is clear he uses various signifyin(g) strategies, including some exaggeration, to establish his persona.[26] For example, Morton explains that a song he originally titled the "Chicago Blues," was renamed the "Jelly Roll Blues," in honor of his verbal wit. Morton describes a comedy routine between himself and Sammy Russell that effectively uses a rhyming ploy. Russell gets a big laugh from the audience after goading Jelly Roll into asking who Sammy is:

> I finally asked him who was he and he stated to me he was Sweet Papa Cream Puff right out of the Bakery Shop. This seemed to produce a big laugh. So while I was muggin', thought came to me that I better say something about the bakery shop. So I told Sammy he didn't know who I was. And when he asked who was I, I said I was Sweet Papa Jelly Roll, With stove pipes in my hips, And all the women in town was dyin' to turn my damper down.[27]

The name Jelly Roll stuck and was soon applied to his composition, too.

But Jelly Roll Morton demonstrates more than the origin of his name in this sequence. He also gives us a feel for his ability to tell jokes and signify better than Sammy Russell. Morton's skill is further emphasized on the recording because the interviewer, apparently less astute than the original audience, then asks him "What'd ya mean ya had stove pipes in your hips?" Morton replied, "A stove pipe's I don't know, one of those things that's very warm—hot hips." Morton's story-telling strategies are consistent with his skill as a "good talker," and they clearly parallel his abilities as an improvising musician accustomed to competition with other entertainers.

Because Morton's "oral autobiography" became a book edited by Lomax, Morton's claim to authenticity is somewhat unusual. In the recording, Morton tells stories and documents his claims with examples from the keyboard itself. Lomax justified his own role as the scribe for Morton's story by describing the process by which Lomax verified not only Morton's musical but also his verbal sounds:

> When he came barreling into the Music Division of the Library of Congress to set the record straight about the origin of jazz and his part in it, he spoke a prose new to my ear, but as ironic, as charming, and as full of surprises as his composition. (It took me four years of rewriting to render his prose on the page so that at times you can almost hear him talking.) Moreover, Jelly Roll was on fire with his story—of a great city and of one of those rare moments in human time when something genuinely new begins.[28]

Lomax wrote a biography, of course; he did not assist Morton with an autobiography. Still, the overall effect of the text, especially when read in tandem with the Library of Congress recordings, is that of a complex call-and-response process.

For example, Lomax interjects "interludes" throughout the text that elaborate on the sections in which Jelly "speaks" directly to the reader. In these sections, Lomax describes New Orleans history and interviews people who knew Morton. They give Lomax freedom to correct or question some of Morton's assertions; consequently, Lomax constructs a text that is possibly far less egocentric than the one Morton "speaks" on the recordings. Yet, Lomax's authority to set straight Morton's biography is countered when the book is set next to the recordings. Then, Morton's own appeal to the authority of oral performance tradition is demonstrated in the audience's conferral of the name Jelly Roll. Morton's authority is also, literally, "on record," even if later thoroughly mediated by Lomax.

Lomax is the most obviously intrusive amanuensis in these texts, but some of the same impressions are created by George Hoefer's interjections in Willie "the Lion" Smith's account. Sidney Bechet, Louis Armstrong, and Danny Barker all worked with writers and editors, although their voices are not as pronounced as those of Lomax and Hoefer.

It is beyond the scope of this essay to do justice to the significance of the collaborator's influences on written autobiographical texts. But we can assume that many editors mediated oral performances, especially if they were preserved as taped interviews. Nevertheless, establishing the full role of the amanuensis should be only the first stage of analyzing a storyteller's strategy. As the excerpt from Morton suggests, these editors could play a variety of supportive or contested roles in the establishment of a persona.[29]

Whatever the role ultimately played by an amanuensis, Smith, Morton, Bechet, Armstrong, and Barker all created personas out of materials and processes akin to those of music. Each man acknowledged that his musical performances also sometimes depended on the impression he created—not just on his ability as a musician. Smith and Morton, like many stride pianists, paid great attention to their clothing and demeanor. Smith explained that his derby "appealed to me because they were worn by the English, the rabbis, and the members of my Masonic lodge. I found that by pulling the derby down in front it gave me mental poise while in action on the piano. When I was relaxed, I wore it to the side."[30] Smith's clothing was just one part of a distinctive style that he carefully nurtured—one that implied the respectability of "polite" society. Morton made a name for himself by adopting a different but equally evocative appearance—that of a sharp-dressing hustler.

Danny Barker explained that musicians in general knew how to give an audience what it wanted, even if it meant faking a few effects. Barker explained how a "trap" was set to get customers to stay out all night and keep spending money after the 3:00 a.m. curfew:

> I first saw the drama cleverly enacted at the old Nest Club.
> . . . At the door upstairs there was Ross the slick doorman.
> When he rang three loud rings . . . it meant some live prosperous-looking people, a party were coming in.
>
> Like jacks out of a box the band struck up *Lady Be Good.* Everybody went into action; the band swinging, waiters beating on trays, everybody smiling and moving, giving the impression the joint was jumping. . . . The unsuspecting party entered amid finger-popping and smiling staff. ("Make believe we're happy.")[31]

Giving an effective performance in this context required putting on a great act. These same skills were used in the autobiographies under discussion here; early jazzmen fully appreciated the power of good performing for past—and future—audiences.

Sidney Bechet opened his autobiography by relating a story about a man who assumed Bechet had invented jazz. Bechet responded, "But you know, Jazz isn't just me. It isn't just any one person who plays it. There'll always be jazz. It doesn't stop with me, it doesn't stop anywhere." Bechet's approach typified all the autobiographical texts under discussion here. Each tells the story of an early jazz pioneer. Yet each acknowledges, often through the powers of exceptional storytelling, the influence of black history and musical traditions on jazz and its individual practitioners. Louis Armstrong, Sidney Bechet, Jelly Roll Morton, Willie "the Lion" Smith, and Danny Barker all identify the participation of black family members, audiences, and other musicians as voices responded to in their musical journeys. As narrators, the men doubly emphasize the role of black communities as creative reference points because each incorporates distinctive discursive strategies from the African-American oral tradition in his story.

Satchmo, Treat It Gentle, Music on My Mind, Mister Jelly Roll, and *A Life in Jazz* are but a small sample of the first-person narrations available for the study of jazz. But the strategies developed by these outstanding musicians and storytellers can serve as a map for researchers to follow as they traverse the road of jazz scholarship.

Notes

Many people have provided useful comments on earlier drafts of this paper, which was presented at the 1988 Modern Language Association Annual Meeting, In addition to participants in that session, I want to thank Deanna Shemek, Ty Miller, Bill Kenney, Jed Rasula, Dan Horowitz, Helen Lefkowitz Horowitz, Sidney J. Lemelle, and William McDonald.

1. Sidney Bechet, *Treat It Gentle* (New York: Hill and Wang, 1960), 4.

2. In addition to Bechet's, the other autobiographies under discussion in this paper are: Danny Barker, *A Life in Jazz*, ed. Alyn Shipton (New York: Oxford University Press, 1986); Alan Lomax, *Mr. Jelly Roll: The Fortunes of Jelly Roll Morton, New Orleans Creole and "Inventor of Jazz"* (New York: Duell, Sloane and Pearce, 1950); Willie "the Lion" Smith and George Hoefer, *Music on My Mind: The Memoirs of an American Pianist* (New York: Doubleday, 1964); and Louis Armstrong, *Swing That Music* (London: Longmans, Green, 1936) and *Satchmo: My Life in New Orleans* (New York: Prentice-Hall, 1954).

On African-American autobiographical traditions, see Stephen Butterfield, *Black Autobiography in America* (Amherst: University of Massachusetts Press, 1974); William L. Andrews, *To Tell A Free Story: The First*

Kathy Ogren

Century of Afro-American Autobiography, 1760–1865 (Urbana: University of Illinois Press, 1986).

3. Bechet, *Treat It Gentle*, 5.

4. On the journey motif in autobiography, see Susanne Egan, *Patterns of Experience in Autobiography* (Chapel Hill: University of North Carolina Press, 1984). Houston Baker discusses the importance of the road, especially the railroad as a central signifying metaphor in *Blues, Ideology, and Afro-American Literature*. (Chicago: University of Chicago Press, 1984).

5. Armstrong, *Satchmo*, 34. In his biography of Armstrong, James Lincoln Collier speculates that this singing gave Armstrong early ear training. James Lincoln Collier, *Louis Armstrong: An American Genius* (New York: Oxford University Press, 1983), 28. Barker tells the story of the Boozan Kings in Chapter 7 of *A Life in Jazz*.

6. Barker, *My Life in Jazz*, 7. In oral history interviews, Barker elaborated on these themes about the sound of New Orleans. In the William Ransom Hogan Oral History of New Orleans Jazz Collection at Tulane University (hereafter TOHNOJC), Barker described the sounds of steamboat whistles and street vendors by singing into the tape. Barker, interview, *TOHNOJC*, June 18, 1959, and June 30, 1959. In his interview in the collection of oral histories edited by Nat Hentoff and Nat Shapiro (*Here Me Talkin' to Ya* [New York: Dover, 1955], 3), Barker remembered: "One of my pleasantest memories as a kid growing up in New Orleans was how a bunch of us kids, playing, would suddenly hear sounds. It was like a phenomenon, like the Aurora Borealis—maybe. The sounds of men playing would be so clear, but we wouldn't be sure where they were coming from. . . . But that music would come on you any time like that. The city was full of the sounds of music."

7. Smith, *Music on My Mind*, 13.

8. For the story of Morton in the saloon, see Lomax, *Mr. Jelly Roll*, 3–4.

9. Marshall Stearns, *The Story of Jazz* (New York: Oxford University Press, 1956), 33. As in other southern cities, society in New Orleans was racist. Its reputation for tolerance was established by comparison with other cities and was largely an outgrowth of its multicultural and Catholic past.

10. Lomax, *Mr. Jelly Roll*, 12.

11. Bechet, *Treat It Gentle*, 61–76; Barker, *A Life in Jazz*, 24.

12. Bechet, *Treat It Gentle*, 63.

13. Smith, *Music On My Mind*, 66–67.

14. Ibid., 23.

15. Collier, *Louis Armstrong*, 36–45, 56–68.

16. Bechet, *Treat It Gentle*, 72–73.

17. Barker, *A Life in Jazz*, 45.

18. Various scholars have suggested ways in which we can best un-

derstand the social and cultural significance of "men of words." In anthropology and folklore, see Roger Abrahams, *Deep Down in The Jungle* (Chicago: Aldine Publishing Co., 1970); Abrahams, *Afro-American Folk Tales: Stories from Black Traditions in the New World* (New York: Pantheon, 1985); and Abrahams, *The Man-of-Words in the West Indies* (Baltimore: Johns Hopkins University Press, 1983). In linguistics, see J. L. Dillard, *Lexicon of Black English* (New York: Seabury Press, 1977), esp. chap. 4; Geneva Smitherman, *Talkin and Testifyin* (Detroit: Wayne State University Press, 1986); and John Baugh, *Black Street Speech: Its History, Structure, and Survival* (Austin: University of Texas Press, 1983). In literary criticism, Houston Baker, *Blues, Ideology, and Afro-American Literature: A Vernacular Theory* (Chicago: University of Chicago Press, 1984); and Henry Louis Gates, *The Signifying Monkey: A Theory of Afro-American Literary Criticism* (New York: Oxford University Press, 1986).

19. Bechet, *Treat It Gentle*, chap. 2.

20. John Chilton describes the writing of Bechet's autobiography in *Sidney Bechet: The Wizard of Jazz*, (New York: Oxford University Press, 1987), 290–92. While at least two writers, Joan Williams and John Ciardi, helped Bechet with the text, Chilton indicates that Bechet was an active participant in shaping the persona that finally emerged in *Treat It Gentle*.

21. Houston Baker, in his *Modernism and the Harlem Renaissance* (Chicago: University of Chicago Press, 1987), draws on the work of anthropologist Richard Price to give this reading to central African-American texts. See, in particular, chap. 8.

22. Smith, *Music On My Mind*, 1–2.

23. Barker, *A Life in Jazz*, chap. 10 and 24.

24. Bechet, *Treat It Gentle*, 1; Smith, *Music On My Mind*, 1–2, 118.

25. Barker, *A Life in Jazz*, vi.

26. I am indebted to the discussions and definitions of signifying provided by the many scholars noted earlier. In particular, Henry Louis Gates's chapter "The Signifying Monkey and the Language of Signifying," from *The Signifying Monkey*, theorizes how "signifyin(g) . . . , means in black discourse modes of figuration themselves" (52).

27. Library of Congress recording.

28. Lomax, *Mr. Jelly Roll*, x.

29. William H. Kenney, III, explores the various roles performed by editors and amanuenses in the autobiographical acts of Louis Armstrong in his essay in this volume. Kenney's observations are applicable to most other jazz autobiographies.

30. Smith, *Music On My Mind*, 47–50.

31. Barker, *A Life in Jazz*, 134.

JAZZ and MODERNISM: CHANGING CONCEPTIONS of INNOVATION and TRADITION

Mark S. Harvey

Jazz from its inception has been perceived as an exemplary expression of the modernist impulse in American culture. Yet its deep roots in the Afro-American folk tradition and its persistent location within the urban popular entertainment context as well as the dynamics of the modernist movement itself have shaped the development of jazz in significant ways. Innovation, the sine qua non of modernism, has undergone important shifts in meaning with respect to the jazz tradition.

I wish to explore these shifts and therefore the various ways in which jazz and modernism have been related. I use three periods as focal points: first, a fairly broad period beginning at about the turn of the century through the 1920s when jazz most explicitly carried the modernist spirit here and abroad and when its innovations challenged the old order of Western music and culture; second, the decade of the 1940s when jazz experienced its first major internal upheaval with the advent of bebop, causing innovation within the jazz tradition; and finally, the period from the late 1950s through the 1960s when one modernist wing sought to make common cause with the then-contemporary "classical" movement and another recovered both the early modern political sense of the term "avant-garde" and various spiritual and cultural resources from non-Western traditions. Having traced this historical course, I conclude by attempting to analyze and interpret the present period, often termed postmodern, in which jazz finds itself in a different place on the cultural landscape from where it began; yet it is enveloped by a climate perhaps not so different with influences from folk sources, urban popular musics, and a general electicism in the ascendant.

By modernism, I mean that broad, monumental shift in the arts and the cultural sensibility of the West datable roughly from around 1890 and perhaps most succinctly characterized by Joseph Wood Krutch as "the modern temper"—a new outlook on both manners and morals.[1] Paralleling and often expressing, while being shaped by, other major forces at work in society such as urbanization, industrialization, and critical social thought and science, modernism emerged as the operative world view for the new century.[2] Yet its debt to romanticism was profound, if generally unacknowledged.[3] Indeed, most determinants of the new sensibility were to be located in some fashion in that of the preceding period; their clearest expression was in the realm of the arts.

Notions of the artist as a unique and unconventional figure bearing the mantle of creator prospered and fostered a heightened sense of individuality and subjectivity.[4] Art for its own sake, as subversive or revolutionary and as spiritual or moral, continued to appeal to various publics albeit in new ways.[5] Most tellingly, the new artistic spirit was ahistorical and antitraditional, quite determinedly pursuing innovation and novelty for its own sake. The freedom to experiment demanded liberation from the approaches and conventions of the past, casting the modern artist as a rebel and a challenger of the arts establishment and the bourgeouis culture of which it was a part.[6] Paradoxically, numerous artists and art movements would eventually challenge aspects of modern culture itself as time passed and the era that had promised so much increasingly frustrated an implicit idealism and prophetic task.

This characterization of what Matei Calinescu has called "aesthetic modernity" generally describes the modernist impulse.[7] Yet many and varied perspectives on modernism depend on the particular ideological, disciplinary, or methodological framework from which it is analyzed and interpreted. Marxist aestheticians, phenomenological reception theorists, proponents of semiotics, structuralism, and deconstructionism all offer their particular points of view, often in competition and conflict with each other.[8] Indeed, the whole enterprise of modernism may have reached a stage where the critics and criticism have replaced artists and artistic activity as its dominant elements.[9] However, important questions about the meaning and value of the arts to larger social, economic, and cultural issues and contexts demand that the critics be taken seriously, if advisedly. Carl Schorske, John Willett, Andreas Huyssen, and Jean-Francois Lyotard, to name only a few, enlighten our understanding of the past and present as they seek to raise our consciousness about the trajectory of our current culture, whether it be termed modern or postmodern.[10]

Music and Modernism

Modernist theory has been dominated by critical approaches drawn from literary and artistic criticism. And although a new emerging field of critical theory dares to be eclectic and interdisciplinary, music tends to be left out of the discussion. Theodor W. Adorno was, of course, one of the first serious critics of musical modernism, and some more recent scholars operating from different viewpoints have included Jacques Attali and Robert P. Morgan.[11] Historical studies by Frederick R. Karl, Richard Shead, and Roger Shattuck have placed musical movements and personages among the main currents of modernism; Leonard B. Meyer has addressed important connections between music and larger cultural issues, and Richard Leppert, Susan McClary, and others have probed the political dimension of music's relationship to society.[12] Yet in comparison with voluminous studies of modernism from the literary and visual arts perspectives, music seems a poor relation.

And with the extant studies, the Adorno bias toward high culture—that is, toward the representative men of modern music like Schoenberg—is pervasive. Shead and Shattuck on the other hand recognize the importance of popular or mass culture expressions such as the cafe, cabaret, music hass, and jazz for early modernism, especially in connection with the Dadaist movement. Attali and American writers like John Rockwell, John Schaefer, and Gunther Schuller exemplify a new trend acknowledging the diversity of the contemporary scene and erasing old divisions between high and popular art.[13] What of jazz—where does this art form, which evolved from folk and popular entertainment sources, fit? And how does it figure in the debate over modernism and postmodernism?

Jazz and Modernism

In this essay I address these questions or at least suggest an outline of the relationship between jazz and modernism. While jazz evolved simultaneously with modernism, and therefore may certainly be termed a "modern" music owing to its historical situation, it has not always partaken of the modernist spirit. And even when doing so, the jazz tradition has selectively manifested various attributes of that movement. Likewise, jazz performers, enthusiasts, and the general public have exhibited a range of attitudes toward jazz as an expression of the modernist impulse.

The literature on this topic is scant indeed. Charles Nanry has dealt with it illuminatingly from a sociological point of view, although his sense of modernism is closer to that of modernization and thus a far different concept than the one with which I am concerned.[14] Berndt Ostendorf has written an intriguing essay on "Anthropology, Modernism, and Jazz," with reference to the work of Ralph Ellison.[15] And comparisons of jazz with the visual arts have been made.[16] Finally, in terms of the context within which jazz and modernism might be profitably considered, several essays in a recent issue of *American Quarterly* should be mentioned;[17] they are important not so much because they take some notice of jazz but because they examine American modernism so well.

While this catalogue of sources is suggestive rather than exhaustive, it does indicate the need for some more general view of the topic. Ted Gioia's recent volume *The Imperfect Art: Reflections on Jazz and Modern Culture* does much to elaborate themes and issues relevant to such an overview, and at many points, his thinking and mine are complementary although I do not agree with every position he takes.[18]

Here I offer another perspective on a general framework by which to consider jazz and modernism, understood in the broad sense I have outlined above, especially in terms of the historical development of jazz. I occasionally use the term "avant-garde" to indicate a particular moment of breakthrough, but I do not equate it with the modernist project as a whole; it is an important dynamic therein, but needs to be differentiated from the larger notion of modernism.[19]

Changing Conceptions of Innovation and Tradition

While a number of approaches to analyzing and interpreting the relationship of jazz and modernism might be suggested, I have chosen one grounded in the changing conceptions of innovation and tradition. Although modernism elevated innovation to the level of a primary aesthetic principle and sought release from perceived limitations of tradition, jazz has always valued both its sources and its evolving tradition.[20] And while innovation within prescribed stylistic categories and approaches has been an estimable, even necessary, aspect of this music, the innovation that challenged basic assumptions and received conventions has been controversial. And precisely this kind of innovation has assured the dynamic growth of jazz, forced periodic reassessments of the tradition, and quite clearly borne the modernist spirit into the world of jazz.

1900 Through the 1920s

The period beginning at the turn of the new century and continuing through the 1920s is germinal. Here multiple strands of the Afro-American folk and popular entertainment traditions—the blues, social dance and brass band music, "ragged-time" minstrel and vaudeville tunes, and the more formal classic ragtime of Joplin and others—experienced an intense blending in the melting pot and cauldron that was New Orleans. This phenomenon did not begin there solely, nor was it limited to that locale; but it did crystallize most brilliantly in that setting. In the urban North, especially in New York, the syncopated dance orchestras of James Reese Europe and others played less from the vernacular and more from the cultivated tradition approach. Yet the substitution of "syncopated" for "social" dance music indicated at least a partial conceptual change in the music making of these players, a tendency that would become more pronounced as southern black musicians made their way northward.

The New Orleans tradition, as we know, was not originally

described by the term jazz. It was a rich musical and cultural complex, part and parcel of the life of the community. Elements of a West African aesthetic transformed by the Afro-American experience pervaded it—the emphasis on process versus product; the notion of creation in time, if not of time itself; the celebration of multiplicity and simultaneity; the balance and appreciation of individual and collective activity, the former often occurring within the latter; and the balance of spontaneity and fixed forms.[21]

The music that would gradually become known to the world as jazz shared this aesthetic with the larger Afro-American cultural tradition. As played by the many brass bands or by the smaller combinations led by Kid Ory and King Oliver, this jazz style was based on collective improvisation and a repertoire of sound images given by the folk and popular entertainment fields. The roles of the various instruments were well defined as were the parameters within which improvisation could take place.

Louis Armstrong and his generation, born around 1900, began to challenge this tradition. These "ear men," as they were called, seemed not to want to be held to the conventions, including printed notation, that the "readers" or "musicianers" insisted upon.[22] A new spirit had entered the music, one prone to innovation. "Papa Joe" Oliver found himself reminding the young Satchmo to play the lead, to maintain a strong melodic statement, even in paraphrase, as was the New Orleans tradition. By the mid-1920s, Armstrong had developed his innovative bent into a new conception, that of the individual solo based on harmonic as much as melodic resources. This was probably due to a variety of factors including his soloistic playing with blues singers, his stint with the Fletcher Henderson band as a featured soloist, and his own imaginative fire. Yet this movement toward individual expression in the improvised solo, now balanced against group polyphony and increasingly contrasted with the more arranged, homophonic ensemble passages, also was a key dynamic of modernism. Louis and the others who participated in this innovative shift away from the established tradition were manifesting something of the modern temper, however unconscious of it they may have been.

In New York, James Reese Europe, having achieved great fame as the music director and bandleader for the celebrated dance duo Vernon and Irene Castle before the Great War and perhaps even greater notice as the leader of the 369th Infantry Hell Fighters Band, which served as regimental band to Allied Commander General

Pershing, found a curious situation upon his return to the United States. Oliver and Armstrong were neither widely known nor recorded, but an all-white quintet from New Orleans calling themselves the Original Dixieland Jazz (ODJB) Band had taken his city, the rest of the country, and parts of Europe by storm. This "jass," as introduced by the ODJB in 1917, became a dominant aspect of the culture of modernism; within a few years it became a primary metaphor for the decade F. Scott Fitzgerald christened as "The Jazz Age." By 1919, James Reese Europe had recorded "Clarinet Marmalade," a piece written and made popular by the ODJB, and was struggling to turn a precision military band cum syncopated dance orchestra into something resembling a jazz band.[23] Yet shortly after Europe's untimely demise, a colleague of his, J. Tim Brynn, warned the all-black musical society known as the Clef Club to "follow their orchestrations more closely and not try so much of their 'ad lib' stuff. There is a growing tendency to make different breaks, discords, and other things which make a lot of noise and jumble up the melody until it is impossible to recognize it."[24] The spirit of innovation in the guise of spontaneous experiment and alteration of a received tradition different from that of New Orleans had manifested itself here as well.

While these kinds of innovation were an important internal dynamic for the development of jazz, the larger significance of jazz for modernism was its cultural symbolism. In this context, jazz was regarded in the popular mind and in that of the intelligentsia as well as a relatively undifferentiated body of lively, rhythmically exciting, urban entertainment music. This music, termed novelty music or "nut jazz" in the early part of this period, constituted a frontal assault on Western culture. The guardians of the establishment blamed this notion of jazz and its concommitant evil, dancing, for most ills of the early twentieth century. A typical critique was published in the August 1921 *Ladies Home Journal*—"Does Jazz Put the Sin in Syncopation?"[25] Of course, the younger, modern generation took a different and decidedly affirmative view of this new social force and typically would have given an enthusiastically affirmative answer to the *Journal* author's question. For youth of the 1920s recognized jazz as a musical expression of a more general trend toward liberation of feeling and life-style away from traditional strictures.[26]

Furthermore, many European modernists regarded this popular jazz movement as highly significant. Often the music was viewed as "exotic" or "primitive" in the same way that Gauguin or Picasso had seen a pure, naive quality in non-Western subject matter or sculpture. For Picabia and other Dadaists, America could also be a source of inspiration as they wondered at "such exotics as the cowboy, jazz, skyscrapers, machines and silent films."[27] With Darius Milhaud's jazz-influenced score for the ballet based on African creation myths collected by poet Blaise Cendrars with sets designed by artist Ferdinand Leger, "The Creation of the World," a combination of the exotic and primitive appeals was achieved.[28]

And a similar perspective obtained among that portion of the white public in America during the Harlem Renaissance who were aware of the black cultural phenomenon. Duke Ellington and his Jungle Band at the Cotton Club in Harlem offered "primitivist" spectacles for the entertainment of a well-heeled clientele seeking the exotic, uptown above Central Park. Ironically, in that setting Ellington began to develop his unique tonal language that would become a hallmark of creative expression in this century.[29]

Jazz, or jazz-as-popular music, then, expressed many aspects of the modernist philosophy; yet in terms of its own aesthetic tradition jazz was only gradually experiencing innovation. However much the early genius of Armstrong and Ellington may have been apparent, they were not perceived as modern artists. And their music was emblematic of the modern mood for the very reason that it was not art, but rather popular, even exotic or primitive, cultural expression.

The 1940s

The next important period in which jazz and modernism may be seen in relationship is the decade of the 1940s. Following the misery of the Depression, America began to slowly recover momentum and so did the jazz business, for this is what it had become. The middle to late 1930s saw the boom of the Swing Era, another popular musical phenomenon not always identifiable with jazz but certainly derivative from it to a greater or lesser extent. Toward the very end of the 1930s and throughout the 1940s, the modernist impulse to innovation surfaced again. This time as before, young black men in their twenties—Charlie Parker, Dizzy Gillespie, Thelonius Monk, and others—sought new directions for the music. However, this time, unlike the previous period of change, innovation occurred within the structural system of the music itself and clearly separated the jazz tradition from that of popular entertainment.

As has often been noted, this watershed point in the history of jazz—the advent of bebop—was both evolutionary and revolutionary, although at the time the latter perception dominated.[30] Familiar harmonic patterns or chord changes were taken as starting points, and then elaborate substitutions for and alterations of parts of those frameworks were made. Familiar melodies were discarded in favor of original, more sinuously complex ones whose rhythmic character was quite intricate. A smaller performing ensemble became the norm, allowing expanded opportunity for the improvisation that the big bands of the Swing Era had frustrated. The roles of each player also expanded so that while a front-line melodic team of horn players and supportive rhythm section configuration remained in place, the rhythm players especially began to weave a more interactive web of countermelody, accent, and harmony in closer dialogue with the soloist than had been the practice previously. Faster tempos, virtuosic displays of technical prowess, new dissonances, and often jagged phrases employing unusual intervals and off-beat punctuation all combined to winnow the audience for this new "modern jazz."

Bebop was the first authentically modern phase in jazz. Experiment and a sense of risk—innovation for its own sake in the cause of advancing the music—marked this development. It also challenged both the entertainment industry and the dancing public and confronted them with an artistically self-conscious listening music. To all but the initiated, this cultural form appeared to be moving away from a connection with the older tradition and toward an autonomous position.[31]

Paradoxically, the modernist musicians themselves—to whom that precise term was increasingly applied—saw themselves, in fact, reclaiming a connection with the older tradition that swing, especially through the white and more diluted, commercial bands, had blurred. Energy, spontaneity, and a sense of created time, against the constraints of fixed large ensemble arrangements, were a legacy from the Afro-American aesthetic. Meanwhile, increased freedom of individual soloistic expression built on the innovations of Armstrong nearly twenty years earlier.

Bop was also a self-conscious attempt to exclude white musicians, at least at first, and to reassert the importance of the black musician, but on artistic rather than entertainment terms.[32] Still,

136

the popular press chose to lionize Dizzy Gillespie—he of the beret, goatee, and tilted trumpet. Despite Gillespie's ability to clown one moment in front of his celebrated (and atypical) bop big band and then deliver a breathtaking exhibition of advanced improvisational mastery, the aberrancies of life-style tended to influence the public's perception of him and the music.

With the avant-garde style, more demanding on players and audiences alike, jazz became differentiated from the world of popular entertainment and spawned a subculture comprised of those who were hip, those who wanted to be hip, and eventually the beatniks, most of whom felt jazz to be the operative metaphor for both life and art. Largely white, this group saw itself, in Norman Mailer's descriptive prose, as "a new breed of adventurers, urban adventurers who drifted out at night looking for action with a black man's code to fit their facts. The hipster had absorbed the existentialist synapses of the Negro [sic] and for practical purposes could be considered a white Negro."[33] As a cultural symbol then, bebop became the metaphor for an esoteric subculture rather than the essence of a whole decade as had been the case previously with the Jazz Age and the Swing Era. Thus, the 1940s provided the setting for a self-conscious and artistically innovative strain to be introduced into the jazz tradition, alienating it from older styles more imbedded in popular song forms and conventions and from a mass audience.

The Late 1950s Through the 1960s

In the 1950s, jazz appeared resurgent in the culture. The festival tradition began at Newport, Rhode Island, in 1954 network television programmed jazz, newspapers commented on the music while the Voice of America beamed it behind the Iron Curtain, and Dizzy Gillespie and Louis Armstrong both made tours abroad as goodwill ambassadors. Yet creative persons within the jazz tradition were content neither to simply replicate proven styles nor to ignore the musical and social implications of bebop.

Toward the latter part of the 1950s and continuing through the 1960s, two major modernist developments occurred; both responded to problems of form and tradition but expressed them in different ways. These were the Third Stream and Free Jazz movements.

Third Stream was innovative on its face, seeking some new

synthesis of the European and jazz traditions. Historically jazz had been a blend of sources from the first, and the symphonic jazz trend of the 1920s or the progressive jazz experiments of the 1940s anticipate what came to be called Third Stream music.[34] Another dynamic at work was the need to create new forms, especially in light of both the advances of improvisers and the apparent exhaustion of theme and variations approaches. Composers capable of inventive arranging and orchestration as well as those having the ability and the desire to conceive new structures were required.

The promise of this Third Stream movement went unfulfilled to a large extent, although some notable experiments succeeded quite well.[35] Often an earlier European form or style was adapted for jazz interpretation or the importation of orchestral instruments into a jazz band sufficed to lend a veneer of prestige or, as was often the case, pretension. More successful were those ventures that sought to assimilate both a contemporary jazz and a contemporary classical approach within a form that was perhaps not quite identifiable with either. By far the major problem seemed to be a diminution or a dilution of the improvisatory aspect coupled with a reticence to use the drums (or the entire rhythm section for that matter) in creative ways. The net effect was that in most cases Third Stream became a kind of jazz variation or mutation of the First Stream, the European classical tradition. However, this movement raised the possibility that jazz musicians could and should be taken seriously as artists.

The Free Jazz movement, by contrast, conceived of innovation in terms of both a radically new aesthetic and a radical reclaiming of the larger cultural tradition of which the jazz tradition was a part. It was also perhaps the most truly "modern" of all the developments in jazz considered here.

Free Jazz—or the New Thing, New Music, Creative Music, or simply the Avant-Garde—enjoyed an extremely wide spectrum of approaches to music making within it.[36] Indeed, it may be too broad a label to properly term a style. Yet the players shared an interest in creating new forms, often through a group process, collective improvisatory approach. An aesthetic of interaction that often eschewed a background-foreground or soloist-accompanist model and an aesthetic of implication that demanded maximum concentration by the listener and required depth immersion beneath the surface of the music was paramount. Instruments were stretched to their limits as was the nature of sound itself. Finally, the accepted common practice of jazz in virtually every respect was either transformed or discarded. This radical conception of music making understandably provoked even more controversy than had the earlier bebop experiments.

Yet there was also present a desire to reclaim elements of the broader cultural tradition underlying jazz, those the jazz tradition itself had obscured. The reappropriation of the collective process, albeit in a new manner, was indicative. Another indicator was the awareness that sound participated in the power, force, and energy of the universe. The Afro-American vocal tradition with its exuberance, supposed roughness or harshness (from a cultivated tradition standpoint), and essential human, emotional expressiveness appealed also. Prodded by attempts of the 1950s to recover the roots of jazz through soul-funk inflections and mannerisms, the avant-gardists of the 1960s made a more thorough-going search amid the inventory of available resources. It was almost as if these exploratory archeologists of sound decided to largely ignore the jazz tradition as it had developed from 1920 to 1960 and to look instead to New Orleans, backward in history through the Afro-American experience and beyond to its roots on the African continent.

In this view eastward and backward, temporally speaking, the intent was not to flirt with the exotic or archaic but rather to discover a new depth perspective on the spiritual and aesthetic dimensions of the black experience. John Coltrane looked even farther eastward, to India as well as to Africa, in his personal quest for truth and inner peace, leaving behind his musical impressions of that pilgrimage and quest. In this, he was very much like the early modern, and the Romantics before them, who had been fascinated with the cultures of Asia and Africa. Others like Albert Ayler sought the spiritual amid the urban, material world, promulgating through fierce, raw sonic preachments rooted in the black church the message that "Music Is the Healing Force in the Universe."[37] Both Coltrane and Ayler seemed to be expressing the sense of the theologian Paul Tillich's analysis of the modern religious consciousness—that it "must find itself again, without the aid of any definite symbolism, in a pure, mystic immediacy."[38]

The new or free music was also frequently concerned with social and political issues, as had been other modernist art movements. Charles Mingus, whose experiments presaged many later developments in Free Jazz, also intimated the rising social consciousness among musicians with his "Fables of Faubus," a lament of outrage sparked by the Civil Rights movement and in particular, one ugly incident in Little Rock, Arkansas. Archie Shepp carried this social concern into a more overtly political one as he directed his music, poetry, and playwriting toward expressing the power of the black experience and its musical tradition on its own terms.

Fundamentally, all these musicians in various ways were calling for nothing less than a cultural revolution, one in which their music would rise above *techne* and tradition to some empyrean heights where it might transform individuals and society. At the very least it would challenge the social and economic structures in which it was embedded and demand both freedom of expression and control of the means of production and distribution.

Never before had jazz musicians achieved such degrees of sophistication and self-awareness about their roles as modern artists and about their work, which was termed art music or black classical music. Regardless of its reinterpretations of traditional or non-Western elements, the "new thing" was clearly based on a new aesthetic with as many inflections as there were performers. And it was absolutely unique—dedicated to the continual reinvention of itself, informed by the urge to innovate and unashamed to reappropriate tradition in the service of creating its future.[39]

The Postmodern Dilemma of the 1980s and Beyond

If jazz was seen in the 1920s as the exemplification of the modernist spirit rebelling against the Western cultivated art tradition, in the 1940s as a bebop revolution within the jazz tradition, and in the 1960s as a free jazz declaration of independence from that jazz tradition, then the 1980s may come to be seen as a time when the innovative dynamic within jazz confronted a dilemma, one that extends into our own time as well. The postmodern dilemma faced by virtually every modernist art form involves once more the relationship of innovation and tradition.

From my perspective, postmodernism is connected to the modernist tradition and shares much of its sensibility.[40] Innovation is still the primary aesthetic principle. And with the mixing of artistic and technological media and the breaking of boundaries between high, popular, folk, and mass art styles, attitudes, and audiences, innovative art has become something of a trendy entertainment medium. "Innovative" or "new" have replaced the term "avant-garde," which almost no artist in any discipline uses anymore. It remains to be seen whether this development has vitiated the role of the arts as prophetic and critical. Playful ironic commentary may have displaced protest and the will for transformation or transcendence of the present order, especially as artistic experiences increasingly become consumer products.

The music we call jazz can happily accept its partially institutionalized position as an art form with authentic claims to that title, or it can exercise the freedom of creative imagination to challenge its own nascent orthodoxy and seek further innovation. Some jazz artists have managed to reconcile the two positions without much compromise, but the dangers of retreat to neoclassicism or of absorption into romanticism are real.[41] If to some degree the avant-garde has become the academy, as Robert Hughes has suggested in connection with the visual arts,[42] then it is the responsibility of artists in every medium to maintain the modernist principles of challenge and innovation lest complacency and ennervation set in.[43]

Jazz has always been a music of individual expression created within a collective context. This balance and the other balance of innovation and tradition, including an awareness of the music's cultural roots and its essential nature as a music of spontaneity and feeling within form, constitute resources to which modern jazz musicians can look for guidance as they encounter postmodern American culture. The humanizing and visionary work of the artists themselves should be the focus of our attention.[44]

Various strategies abound, drawing on a general aesthetic of eclecticism. Don Cherry travels the globe listening to and playing with musicians from many cultures. The Art Ensemble of Chicago and Sun Ra's Arkestra invoke premodern spirits to invent new rituals that are entertaining even as they are profound. The Ganelin Trio and other Soviet jazz musicians reintroduce aspects of vaudeville and humor into their performances of high intensity improvisation, while Ran Blake, Anthony Davis, and Anthony Braxton, among others, chart new directions for a reinterpretation of the Third Stream ideal, synthesizing improvisation and composition into strikingly original worlds of sound. And composers as diverse as Henry Threadgill, George Russell, Ornette Coleman, Geri Allen, Carla Bley, and Butch Morris continue to reshape the jazz tradition in their own unique ways.

As Martin Williams has noted, the jazz tradition is in a period of synthesis or summary, a relatively conservative period of retrenchment but not necessarily of stagnation.[45] As evidenced by the list of artists and groups mentioned above, there is much vitality about. And if few coherent styles or schools seem to have emerged and if few marked breakthroughs appear to have occurred, I share Williams's optimism that eventually it will happen as it has happened before.

Notes

1. Joseph Wood Krutch, *The Modern Temper* (New York: Harcourt, Brace & Co., 1929).

2. Stephen Kern, *The Culture of Time and Space: 1880–1918* (London: Weidenfeld and Nicolson, 1983). This is a truly remarkable synthesis of the disparate changes occuring in this formative period.

3. Renato Poggioli, *The Theory of the Avant-Garde*, trans. Gerald Fitzgerald (Cambridge: Belknap Press/Harvard University Press, 1968), see esp. chap. 3.

4. For a stimulating investigation of this conception of the artist, see Ernst Kris and Otto Kurz, *Legend, Myth, and Magic in the Image of the Artist: A Historical Experiment* (New Haven: Yale University Press, 1979).

5. For an exploration of these themes in romanticism and modern art, see Jacques Barzun, *The Use and Abuse of Art* (Princeton: Princeton University Press/ Bollingen Series XXV, 1975). Cf. Poggioli on the transformation of these and other romanticist themes in art of the modern period.

6. Irving Howe, *The Idea of the Modern in Literature and Arts* (New York: Horizon Press, 1967).

7. Matei Calinescu, *Five Faces of Modernity: Modernism, Avant-Garde, Decadence, Kitsch, Postmodernism* (1977; Durham, N.C.: Duke University Press, 1987), 3–10.

8. Terry Eagleton has provided a succinct summary of the principal methodological strategies in his *Literary Theory: An Introduction* (Minneapolis: University of Minnesota Press, 1983). These include phenomenology, hermeneutics, reception theory; structuralism and semiotics; poststructuralism; and psychoanalysis. While focused on literary criticism, they are not limited to that field. In fact, what has been emerging recently is a new field of critical theory indebted to literary criticism but ranging

across disciplinary boundaries and often drawing on various of these and other theories. Other perspectives on literary modernism may be found in Malcolm Bradbury and James McFarlane, eds., *Modernism: 1890–1930* (Hammondsworth, Eng.: Penguin Books, 1976), esp. the editors' chap. "The Name and Nature of Modernism," and Robert Kiely, ed., *Modernism Reconsidered* (Cambridge: Harvard University Press, 1983). For the visual arts, see Robert Hughes, *The Shock of the New* (New York: Knopf, 1982), and Rosalind Krauss, *The Originality of the Avant-Garde and Other Modernist Myths* (Cambridge: MIT Press, 1986). By contrast, see the earlier critical stance with respect to modernism in Clement Greenberg, *Art and Culture* (Boston: Beacon Press, 1961).

9. This notion surfaces from time to time in various places, but I encountered it first-hand as a participant in a National Endowment for the Humanities Summer Institute for the Study of Avant-Gardes at Harvard University during the summer of 1987. Someone actually stated aloud that perhaps the critics had become the new avant-garde. Perhaps that is true, or perhaps there is such collusion between critics and artists, especially would-be avant-gardists, that one category cannot exist without the other.

10. Schorske in *Fin-de-Siecle Vienna: Politics and Culture* (New York: Vintage Books/Random House, 1981), and Willett in *Art and Politics in the Weimar Period: The New Sobriety, 1917–1933* (New York: Pantheon, 1978) focus on earlier historical moments. Huyssen in *After the Great Divide: Modernism, Mass Culture, Postmodernism* (Bloomington: Indiana University Press, 1986) and his opposite Lyotard in *The Postmodern Condition: A Report on Knowledge*, trans. Geoff Bennington and Brian Massumi (1979; Minneapolis: University of Minnesota Press, 1984) present analyses of the contemporary situation in terms of the current critical debate.

The term "postmodernism" is at least as problematic and elusive as is modernism. Some, like Huyssen, see it as continuation of modernism, with new emphases, while others, like Krauss and most writers represented in Hal Foster's collection of essays (*The Anti-Aesthetic: Essays on Postmodern Culture* [Port Townsend, Wash.: Bay Press, 1983]) see it as sharply differentiated from the modernist project. For a penetrating critique of the whole cultural-critical debate that inveighs against all parties, see Charles Newman, *The Post-Modern Aura: The Act of Fiction in an Age of Inflation* (Evanston, Ill.: Northwestern University Press, 1985).

11. Theodor W. Adorno, *Introduction to the Sociology of Music*, trans. E. B. Ashton (1962; New York: Seabury Press, 1976). While Adorno represented the viewpoint of the Frankfurt School, Attali is indebted to him yet post-Adorno, post-structuralist, and post-Marxist in his treatise *Noise: The Political Economy of Music*, trans. Brian Massumi (1977; Minneapolis: University of Minnesota Press, 1985). Morgan in "Secret Languages: the Roots of Musical Modernism," *Critical Inquiry* 10, no. 3 (March 1984): 442–

61, presents a structural-theoretical analysis—in musical terms—in search of a new metaphorical understanding of the "language(s)" of the musical art.

12. Frederick R. Karl, *Modern and Modernism: The Sovereignty of the Artist, 1885–1925* (New York: Atheneum, 1985); Richard Shead, *Music in the 1920s* (New York: St. Martin's, 1976); and Richard Shattuck, *The Banquet Years: The Origins of the Avant-Garde in France 1885 to World War I*, rev. ed. (New York: Vintage Books/Random House, 1968). Leonard B. Meyer, *Music, the Arts, and Ideas: Patterns and Predictions in Twentieth-Century Culture* (Chicago: University of Chicago Press, 1967); and Richard Leppert and Susan McClary, eds., *Music and Society: The Politics of Composition, Performance and Reception* (Cambridge, Eng.: Cambridge University Press, 1987).

13. John Rockwell, *All American Music: Composition in the Late Twentieth Century* (New York: Knopf, 1983); John Schaefer, *New Sounds: A Listener's Guide to New Music* (New York: Harper & Row, 1987); and Gunther Schuller, *Musings* (New York: Oxford University Press, 1986). For a general consideration of this issue, see Huyssen, *After the Great Divide.*

14. Charles Nanry, "Jazz and Modernism: Twin-Born Children of the Age of Invention," *Annual Review of Jazz Studies* 1 (1972): 146–54.

15. Berndt Ostendorf, "Anthropology, Modernism, and Jazz," in *Ralph Ellison*, ed. Harold Bloom, (New York: Chelsea House Publishers/Modern Critical Views, 1986), 145–72.

16. Chad Mandeles, "Jackson Pollack and Jazz: Structural Parallels," *Arts Magazine* 56, no. 2 (October 1981): 139–41, illus., and Mona Hadler, "Jazz and the Visual Arts," *Arts Magazine* 57, no. 10 (June 1983): 91–101, illus.

17. Daniel Joseph Singal, "Modernist Culture in America: Introduction," *American Quarterly* 39, no. 1 (Spring 1987): 5–6; Signal, "Towards a Definition of American Modernism," *AQ* 39, no. 1: 7–26; Malcolm Bradbury, "The Nonhomemade World: European and American Modernism," *AQ* 39, no. 1: 27–36; and Houston A. Baker, Jr., "Modernism and the Harlem Renaissance," *AQ* 39, no. 1: 84–97. This whole issue is worth looking at for those interested in American modernism.

18. Ted Gioia, *The Imperfect Art: Reflections on Jazz and Modern Culture* (New York: Oxford University Press, 1988). Many striking insights in this set of essays deal with aesthetics and social analysis. Gioia refers often to the concept of innovation, even playing out the innovation-tradition discussion in various ways and focusing on the main periods that I have chosen.

19. This appears to be the consensus view of critical theorists with Peter Bürger taking a more pronounced position on behalf of the avant-garde as radically differentiated from modernism. See Burger, *Theory of the Avant-Garde*, trans. Michael Shaw (1974; Minneapolis: University of Min-

nesota Press, 1984). I should add that the term "consensus" in this field of inquiry is very slippery.

20. These sources—African, Afro-American, American—and the evolving jazz tradition may be viewed as a continuum. Indeed, this is my position. At the same time, it is possible to note the emergence of a more specific "jazz tradition" beginning, as the consensus holds, around 1890. It is my conviction that only by recognizing both the general tradition and the evolving nature of the more specific one can the fullest understanding of this music known as jazz be possible.

21. For a general discussion of philosophy with implications for aesthetics, see John S. Mbiti, *African Religions and Philosophy* (Garden City, N.Y.: Doubleday/Anchor Books, 1970). For various perspectives on aesthetics in the black experience, see Addison Gayle, Jr., ed., *The Black Aesthetic* (Garden City: N.Y.: Doubleday, 1971). See also Leroi Jones/Amiri Baraka, *Blues People* (New York: William Morrow, 1963).

22. For an enlightening discussion of this whole cultural context, see William J. Schafer, with assistance from Richard B. Allen, *Brass Bands and New Orleans Jazz* (Baton Rouge: Louisiana State University Press, 1977).

23. For recordings by James Reese Europe and an introductory essay in the form of liner notes covering Europe and his period, see the album *Steppin' On the Gas: Rags to Jazz, 1913–1927*, New World Records/NWR 269, Recorded Anthology of American Music, 1977.

24. Quoted in Jim Haskins, *The Cotton Club* (New York: Random House, 1977), 15. The address to the Clef Club was made in June 1921.

25. Quoted in Neil Leonard, *Jazz and the White Americans* (Chicago: University of Chicago Press, 1962), 35. The article appeared in the *Ladies Home Journal*, August 1921, 34; it was written by Anne Shaw Faulkner (Mrs. Marx Obendorfer).

26. Paula S. Fass, *The Damned and the Beautiful: American Youth in the 1920s* (New York: Oxford University Press, 1977).

27. John D. Erickson, *Dada: Performance, Poetry and Art* (Boston: Twayne Publishers, 1984), 31. Also see chap. 2, "In the Land of Jazz, Skyscrapers and Machines: New York Dada," for the seeming confusion (if not identification) of African music and jazz.

28. Milhaud and the others gave the premier of "La Creation du Monde" in October 1923. This predates by several months the composition and premier of Gershwin's "Rhapsody in Blue," yet there are remarkable similarities of sound, especially in the blues-inflected sections, although no direct identity of musical materials is evident.

Many composers from both the European and the American classical tradition were interested in jazz in this period, including Igor Stravinsky, and Debussy (both more influenced by ragtime), Ravel, Hindemith, Weill, Krenek, Antheil, Copland, and others. For a summary of this movement, see Aaron Copland, *The New Music: 1900–1960*, rev. and enl. ed. (New York:

Norton, 1968), 59–74. For brief highlights of musical and other modernist art activities within the wider sphere of culture and politics, see Willett, *Art and Politics in the Weimar Period*. For a discussion of the "primitivist" dynamic, see Gioia, chap. 2.

29. For the Harlem Renaissance, see Nathan I. Huggins, *Harlem Renaissance* (New York: Oxford, 1971), and David L. Lewis, *When Harlem Was in Vogue* (New York: Vintage/Random House, 1979). Haskins, *Cotton Club*, focuses on that club while discussions of Ellington's early music can be found in Gunther Schuller, *Early Jazz* (New York: Oxford University Press, 1968), Peter Gammond, ed., *Duke Ellington: His Life and Music* (1958; New York: DaCapo, 1977), and G. E. Lambert, *Duke Ellington* (1959; New York: A. S. Barnes & Co., 1961).

30. The bebop phenomenon has been well recognized by jazz enthusiasts and more recently by the general musical public. For some sources to consult for those less familiar with this style, see Leonard Feather, *Inside Jazz* (New York: DaCapo, 1977) originally published in 1949 as "Inside Bebop"; Ira Gitler, *Swing to Bop* (New York: Oxford University Press, 1985), an oral history.

31. Gioia, *Imperfect Art*, 119–21.

32. For a good summary discussion of this aspect and the bop period, see Leslie B. Rout, Jr., "Reflections on the Evolution of PostWar Jazz" in *The Black Aesthetic*, 150–57, 140.

33. Norman Mailer, "The White Negro," in *The Beat Generation and the Angry Young Men*, ed. by Gene Feldman and Max Gartenberg (New York: Dell, 1958), 375. This collection also contains work with jazz imagery by Jack Kerouac and Allen Ginsberg as well as Kenneth Rexroth's critical piece comparing Bird with Dylan Thomas.

34. Third Stream was a term coined by Gunther Schuller in the late 1950s. For further reading, see Schuller, *Musings* (New York: Oxford University Press, 1986), 114–33, and Schuller's "Jazz and Classical Music," in *The New Edition of the Encyclopedia of Jazz*, ed. Leonard Feather (New York: Bonanza, 1960).

35. Works commissioned for the famous Brandeis Festival of the Arts Concert by Jimmy Giuffre, Charles Mingus, George Russell, Gunther Schuller, and others are among the best examples of good Third Stream music. Cf. discographical note (Appendix C).

36. Several books provide good overviews of the Free Jazz scene. Among them are Ekkehard Jost, *Free Jazz* (Graz, Austria: Universal, 1974), Valerie Wilmer, *As Serious as Your Life: The Story of the New Jazz* (Westport, Conn.: Lawrence Hall, 1980), and John Litweiler, *The Freedom Principle: Jazz After 1958* (New York: William Morrow, 1984).

37. Wilmer, 110.

38. Paul Tillich, *The Religious Situation*, trans. H. Richard Neibuhr (1932; New York: World Publishing, 1969), 89. For a consideration of jazz

in mythic and religious perspective based in sociocultural analysis rather than theology or philosophy of religion see Neil Leonard, *Jazz: Myth and Religion* (New York: Oxford University Press, 1987).

39. Gioia also notes this penchant for continual reinvention, progress, and the advancement of the art of jazz, but his is a decidedly less affirmative view than mine. He also locates the beginnings of this trend in the bebop movement, a point with which I do not disagree. However, I feel that it was in the 1960s that this dynamic, established earlier in principle and manifested to some degree, really exerted influence in terms of major reconceptualization of form and performance practice, not merely in terms of alterations of extant materials and frameworks.

40. I agree with Huyssen and others on this point and disagree with those who see postmodernism as a radical break with modernism. Cf. note 10 above and two other assessments of his issue: Harry Garvin, ed., *Romanticism, Modernism, Postmodernism* (Lewisburg, Pa.: Bucknell University Press, 1980), and Christopher Butler, *After the Wake: An Essay on the Contemporary Avant-Garde* (London: Clarendon Press/Oxford University Press, 1980).

41. Wynton Marsalis is the leading proponent of neoclassicism both in his music making and in his frequent published comments; cf. Wynton Marsalis, "What Jazz Is—and Isn't," *New York Times*, Sunday, July 31, 1988, pp. 21, 24. Ted Gioia takes note of the incipient orientation toward romanticism in jazz, especially as it pertains to the life-style of the jazz musician, 82ff.

42. Hughes, *Shock of the New*, 392, and chap. 8 for a discussion of the postmodern situation. Not only do art critics and theorists see themselves as the avant-garde (see note 9 above), but also many artists, including many jazz musicians, have become part of the academy.

43. For a general discussion of this viewpoint in terms of black culture, see Cornel West, "Postmodernism and Black America," *Zeta Magazine* (June 1988): 27–29.

44. Again I must note that Ted Gioia addresses the humanizing role of jazz in the face of what he perceives to be the dehumanization of modern art, after Ortega y Gasset. Again I agree with him in part. In my view, the individual must always be seen in the social and cultural context(s) with which he interacts and in which the individual artist's work takes on meaning. Thus, I am not willing to assert the primacy of the individual artist as the hope for the future of jazz, although as my own comments would make clear, I value this element highly.

45. Martin Williams, "How Long Has This Been Going On?" *Jazz Times*, February 1987, 7.

JAZZ as SOCIAL STRUCTURE,
PROCESS, and OUTCOME

David T. Bastien and Todd J. Hostager

Jazz is a recent American art form that embodies modern American values and contemporary reality. It is simultaneously uni-cultural and pluralistic. It represents events, and creative responses to those events, and is not simply a product. As a form, it is designed to be spontaneous, innovative, and constantly novel. In several ways, it addresses the central concerns of organizations and managers. First, jazz is a social form, in that it is performed by a group of players simultaneously improvising. It is self-consciously spontaneous, creative, and expressive. Jazz is produced through a theory and set of social practices that are designed to enable novel and innovative performances by accommodating both individual differences and internal (theoretical and practical) changes. Jazz theories and practice are built on the assumption that each musician is simultaneously and consciously adapting to the whole, supporting the other players, and influencing the outcome. As with all of the arts, the form is also an industry or profession. Those practitioners who work at it professionally and full-time learn the theories and practices more fluently than non-full-time professionals. Therefore, studying how adroit professionals successfully manage the coordination of a creative and innovative process ought to give us some

148

insight into at least one way of managing innovation processes in other contexts. Finally, music in general and jazz in particular are processes with an outcome but no product (except when a recording is made and sold). Because of this, we should be able to identify processes of change and innovation more clearly, without any confounding factors relating primarily to product.

The advent of relatively inexpensive and unobtrusive videotaping technology has allowed the study of actual instances of behavior in context, something not previously possible. One of the newer things it allows us to do is to study events that are not intended to occur again; such things as jazz performances. The authors of this study were able to obtain a complete video-taped record of a jazz concert. It records the musicians from shortly after the time they arrived and met each other until shortly before they left the concert hall. This particular concert was artistically highly credible while having a laboratory-like social construction, in that the four musicians had never worked together as a group, they had no rehearsal, and they had no scores or charts. The critical response to the concert was strong, with the *St. Paul Pioneer Press-Dispatch*, in a year-end review of the concert season, naming it one of the top ten musical events in the Twin Cities.

This essay examines this basic question: what are the means through which a zero-history group, with all of its inherent uncertainty, produces a coordinated and credible product in an essentially turbulent field, such as is presented in the art form of jazz? At this point it must be noted that this is a central question for managers of businesses and other kinds of work organizations (Emery and Trist, 1975). As will be discussed later, coordination of the activity of organizational actors in the face of an unpredictably turbulent economic and business environment presents a conceptual problem for managers because no good social or behavioral models have emerged from the study of business organizations.

The examination of this question in jazz is based on data that were gathered on videotape. The findings and theory will be discussed in comparison with existing social psychological approaches to group jazz performances (e.g., Bougon, Weick, & Binkhorst, 1977; Voyer & Faulkner, 1986a, 1986b; Weick, Gilfillan, & Keith, 1973), and will be extended beyond group improvisation in jazz to group improvisation in organizations and to management strategies that encourage and support innovation. Furthermore, there are new implications for the study of jazz that will be developed. Interestingly, these implications also condition and change the focus of the study of other kinds of organizations and of the study of management in general.

Background of the case

The concert under study, produced by Bob DeFlores and May-time Productions, was performed June 29, 1985, in St. Paul, Minnesota. Maytime Productions is a nonprofit organization created to promote and preserve jazz as a living American art form. The four musicians—Budd Freeman (tenor saxaphone), Art Hodes (piano), Biddy Bastien (bass), and Hal Smith (drums)—represent over two hundred years of professional experience. They had never worked together before as a group, although Freeman and Hodes and Hodes and Bastien had played together under other circumstances. They did not rehearse, did not use written materials (scores, charts, etc.), and met only a few minutes before the show went on. This meets our definition of zero-history: a group of people brought together to accomplish a task that has no history as a group. In bringing such a group together, DeFlores and Maytime arranged the concert so that the entire process of cognitive organizing, musical understanding, and social coordination took place in front of the audience. Unedited tapes of the event were made available to the researchers for the conduct of this study (see Methods section).

This concert presents an extreme form of jazz in at least three ways: (1) the music was performed extemporaneously, that is, without rehearsals, song lists, or charts; (2) the music was socially produced by four simultaneously improvising musicians; and (3) the group had no prior experience together. We can see that the uncertainty presented by the zero-history nature of the group is complemented by the basic turbulence of the art form. Uncertainty is the awareness of not knowing what to expect of the future or of others. Turbulence is defined as "an environment in which there are dynamic processes arising from the field itself which create significant variances for the component systems" (Emery and Trist, 1975:52). While this kind of jazz event is not unusual from the perspective of working musicians, it is unusual to social scientists, who are used to arranging and analyzing relatively certain and placid social phenomena. With this videotaped record we are presented with a successfully completed social task. Again, the entirety of the event was recorded, from only a few minutes after the musicians arrived and met each other until they left the hall.

Jazz in the idealized form of the art of this concert is considerably different from other musical forms in its unique set of characteristics:

1. macro musical structures (at the level of the overall form and song) are prescribed through music theory. The musical rules of the task are prescribed here;

2. group integrating structures are prescribed by the traditions of the profession, especially leadership and communication codes and rules. The organizing rules are prescribed here;

3. improvisation is the assumed and expected mode of individual behavior;

4. the artistic worth and judgments of the event's success are determined by the overall integrated social product;

These very characteristics make jazz, at least of this type, interesting to social scientists because all human organizational performance and behavior shares them in some basic ways. Jazz performances, though, can have laboratory-like controls that are not normally seen in everyday organizational life. In this particular case, the zero-history aspect of the group is a critical control, as are the more than two hundred years of professional experience of the players, ensuring functionally nearly perfect control of the technique and protocols of the form. Another control is the absence of rehearsal or charts. A further control in this case exists in the form of the critical response to the concert; reviews were very positive. This particular type of event, with these controls and fully video-recorded, also allows the study of real social/task processes in a temporally compressed form, thereby seeing these processes clearly and linking them to outcomes, where they might not be visible at all if we were looking at a more "normal time" complete task interaction.

Levels of integrating structures and behaviors

Jazz theory, a set of formal structural conventions used to generate musical concepts, is the first level at which a jazz performance can be evaluated; it is also the first level of structural constraint

151

upon individual behavior. As with all macrostructural constraints, however, the structure enables performance by decreasing uncertainty. As these theories are the stuff of much writing, well-known to all jazz musicians, we do not describe them here other than to note that these theories are theories of chords (assemblies of notes), chordal relationships, and chordal progressions.

Unwritten normative structuring conventions, which serve the purpose of integrating the group, represent the second level. These are not of any necessary theoretical or aesthetic importance, but they allow easier coordination and organization. They are embedded in the profession of jazz. Among the relevant conventions are:

1. the nominal leader (Bud Freeman in this case) calls (decides) the song and the key to be played;
2. whoever is the soloist (dominant voice) at the moment determines the style (time, level of embellishment, etc.), and the others are expected to support the determination;
3. at one point or another, each musician gets the opportunity to be the soloist;
4. the chorus is the basic unit of soloist control unless otherwise specified by the nominal leader.

A part of this second level are the communicative codes that have become traditional among practitioners of the art. Coded communication is here defined as behavior intended to be communicative, relying on arbitrary assignment of meaning to behavior, where the arbitrary assignment has been agreed upon by a community of code users. These codes include both words and phrases that have unique and distinct meaning in the profession, and nonverbal cues that have become traditional, such as turning to an individual, eye contact at particular points, and so on. These cues form a vehicle through which musicians communicate about their performance while the performance is ongoing. They are designed not only for communication to each other but also to be as unobtrusive as possible while being invisible to an audience.

While the codes are to be viewed as a part of the second level of structure (professional/social), their invocation is the third level, which is real, explicit, and observable communicative behavior. The behaviors must be consistent with the upper two levels, and the communication codes themselves are within the second level; however, this third level specifies which of, and when, the various rules will be followed.

As mentioned above, the entire performance was videotaped. Three versions of the tape were made:

1. an edited version, featuring the quartet with Freeman in which all verbal banter between songs was eliminated as were some songs, which were also resequenced (this version is suitable for commercial sale or broadcast);
2. an edited version featuring primarily Hodes, but including some quartet songs. Its song sequence bears no relationship with the actual performed sequence (this version is also for broadcast use);
3. the field-mixed original containing all the live performance in sequence, without entrances or the historic films prefacing each of the three sets of the concert.

The third tape, being the most complete record of the event, was used as one major source of data. The second source was the bass player, Biddy Bastien, who served as a participant observer. Bastien, with the two researchers present, reviewed the tape and explained, and commented on the important organizing and communicative behaviors of all four participants as the performance emerged. From this, a draft of the case was developed and forwarded to the other three musicians along with a copy of the tape for review and comments.

The Performance

The concert was held in a rather large traditional concert hall that was about half full during the performance. Prior to the concert, the four musicians had little time to discuss what would happen. The brief discussion that did occur specified only the following items:

1. the songs called would be standards (presumably known to most jazz professionals);
2. each song would start with a piano introduction, then the tenor would play the melody followed by a couple choruses of improvised solo, the piano would then take a chorus or

two of solo, then either the tenor would pick up the lead again or the bass and drums would alternate on four- or eight-bar breaks;

3. except for Hodes's solo parts, Freeman would call the tunes and their keys;

4. no dragging! (gradually slowing the tempo)

The concert consisted of three sets. The first set was critical from our perspective in that most basic, inherent uncertainty was resolved there. Although each set introduced novelty, in the first set initial operating understandings had to be reached so that further novelty could be realized.

When the players took their places on stage, Freeman called the first song, "Sunday." This is a rather simple song, without much possible stylistic variance. Here we can observe coded communication being redundantly employed, with functional redundancy on three levels. The first level is structurally embedded in the music (chorus endings) followed through the counting of choruses by musicians and sticking with the chorus agreement (above). In this song, the second level was accessed through Freeman's use of the musically theoretical cue of "winding down" the solo. On the third level, there were visual cues in Freeman turning to Hodes shortly (a beat or two) before the end of his solo. Freeman's intent was clearly communicative. During this song, we can also observe that whoever was backing up the soloist was watching the soloist intently. Finally, although it did not appear intentionally communicative, Freeman became more active physically at the points of change of soloist, also helping to focus the attention of the entire group on the changes coming up. At the end of Hodes's solo, Freeman again showed movement and invoked agreement with the bass and drums for "fours" (four-bar breaks) with a questioning look. Both Smith and Bastien nodded in response. It is interesting to note that verbal language, the usual vehicle of coded, intentional communication, was not the communicative medium chosen here; rather, nonverbal signs were preferred.

Following a long bit of banter with the audience, Freeman called the second song, "You Took Advantage of Me," This song has a bit more potential for stylistic variation than the first. Again, the musicians watched each other closely while playing. During his solo, Hodes introduced a bass line that was somewhat unexpected by Bastian, but because of uncertainty of the situation and the heightened attention, Bastien was able to pick up the change and follow it. This helped set up a pattern of changes that would occur later in the concert whenever Hodes was playing. Again, Freeman used visual signals to underscore the changes in soloists, looking at the coming soloists and nodding to them or giving verbal instructions. Freeman called a chorus of "fours" with Smith; then, at the end of the chorus, he said "again," indicating a second chorus.

The third song, "Misty," allowed for considerable stylistic variation, particularly in using embellished chord progressions. Freeman and Hodes both used an unembellished structure that cemented the understandings of all the musicians that this approach to style would be followed throughout the concert. During this set, also, we saw the use of a hand sign to signal changes in time from 4/4 to 2/4 during Hodes's solo. This use of 2/4 time was one regular feature of Hodes's solos throughout the rest of the concert, even though the songs were in 4/4 and the others preferred 4/4 during their solos.

Two songs finished the first set—a Hodes solo piece and an early 1930s standard. The set was marked by sticking to the initial understandings rigidly, the establishment of general preferences for unembellished rather than embellished chords, and the establishment of specific preferences in time by each soloist. The first set also saw the assertion by Freeman of his leadership position through not only calling the songs but also managing the sequences of players. Freeman also asserted his personality, reputed to be highly social and charming, through his shouting of encouragement to the various soloists as they were playing. All the musicians spent much of this set paying considerable sensory attention to the others, both listening and watching.

The second set started with the precedents and preferences already somewhat established. During this set, we saw the change from constant visual attention to the rest of the group to a more selective attention. Because everything was new and surprising during the first set, constant attention was required; during the second set we saw that visual attention was high around the points of change but dropped off somewhat between changes. The overall sound of this set may have been somewhat more satisfactory to the individuals as they "knew" when changes in time and soloist would take place, and the soloists "knew" they would get support without expending much energy into communicating preferences.

Because of this Freeman was able to extend his solo an extra chorus on one song. He recognized that the attention of the others was focused on him, waiting for his musical and other signals. He declined to give signals at the end of his second chorus, so the others simply followed him into a third.

The third and final set started with a long piano solo by Hodes, so the ensemble portion of the set was slightly shorter than the first two. This set saw the patterns, roles, and communicative behaviors of the first two sets repeated and underscored, although the group became increasingly adventurous throughout the performance, inventing the "Twin Cities Blues" late in this last set.

Analysis

Our analysis differs considerably from existing studies of jazz by social scientists. First, we analyze a zero-history group performance unconstrained by charts or any written tools. The other studies featured performances by groups that had practiced together before and largely used sheet music to guide them (see, e.g., Bougon, Weick, & Binkhorst, 1977; Voyer & Faulkner, 1986a, 1986b; Weick, Gilfillan, & Keith, 1976). Obviously, such differences in performance conditions require different musical and social psychological skills, which in turn condition the theoretical representation of the structures and processes through which the group achieved an integrated product. Another major difference is that our analysis focuses on the structural and processual aspects of an actual performance, while the bulk of the existing approaches (viz., Bougan, Weick, & Binkhorst, 1977; Voyer & Faulkner, 1986a, 1986b) have worked to establish a map of perceived causal relationships among variables such as satisfaction with rehearsal, time spent rehearsing, and the quality of performance. Another key difference is that others have explored leadership as an element of group performance, while we are exploring coded communication and attention as means of leading oneself and others. In sum, the existing social science literature has focused on explicating the cognitive relationships undergirding more formally prescribed group jazz performance through questionnaires and statistics, while we have looked at social structures and processes operating in an actual improvisation as recorded on videotape.

Although they are not discussed in this literature, a number of aspects of this specific event would be important to discuss, but they are outside the scope of this essay. The normative role structure and instrumentation are important to explaining this event, as is the physical arrangement of the musicians. The element of individual fame is also an issue that we do not accommodate here, but it played some part in reducing the uncertainty of the situation. Leadership would also be a useful perspective for analysis, but the discussion of these perspectives must wait for future studies. It is important to note, therefore, that a wealth of analysis is available from this single rich, fully recorded, well-controlled case. Furthermore, a number of perspectives (at least those listed above) must be synthesized to fully explain the data from this concert. In this essay only the organizing strategies and tactics will be explained, leaving the necessary broader synthesis for subsequent research.

Multiple Sequence Tracking

Poole, in leaderless task groups, developed the Multiple Sequence Model to relate differing aspects of group task processes (Poole, 1983). This model suggests portraying the group processes as a set of parallel strands or tracks of activity as they emerge over time. Each track represents a different aspect of the process and relates to a different level of data. Among the strengths of this approach to the data is that it allows for analysis of relationships between and across levels. Here it is adapted to our specific purposes through assigning the three parallel tracks—music theory (structure), professional (group) norms, and individual communication. Poole further introduced the important concept of breakpoints, points in time when changes run across all tracks, changing the direction and basic nature of group activity (1983). It must be remembered that the change is from one kind of activity to another kind of activity, and that a central issue for jazz players is knowing when a breakpoint (such as a change in soloist) might be expected and what to expect on the future side of it.

As shown in the multiple sequence tracking in Figure 1, the potential for a change must exist on the levels of jazz theory (macrostructure) and professional norms (integrating structure) before it can be considered by the individual players, but that two-level potential must be explicitly and redundantly invoked by coded

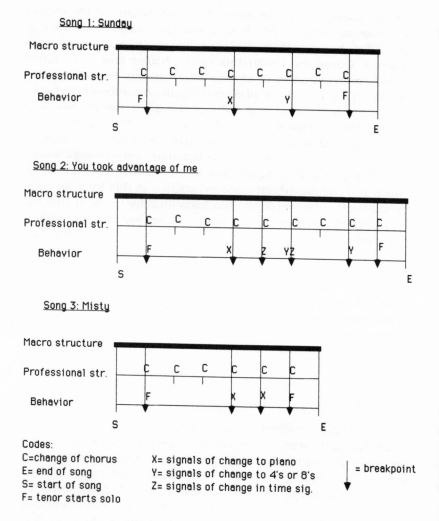

Figure 1. Multiple Sequence Tracking of the first three songs of the first set.

communication at the individual level to become an actual break-point. As we descend from the theoretical (macrostructural) to the normative (integrating structure) to the behavioral level, each level further constrains the available choices, but to change a choice all three levels must be accessed. On the macrostructural track (jazz theory), changes could be made almost anywhere. At the second (professional norms) level, though, changes could only happen at the end of choruses. At the level of explicit communicative behavior, however, within the constraints of the higher levels the actual coded communication of change happens less frequently than possible. This redundancy of communicative behavior across tracks is important, for it captures the attention of the players; and changes do not happen without it.

In the first song, changes were made primarily by the soloist at the end of every two choruses. This pattern emerges as preferred throughout the rest of the concert. In the third song, Hodes introduced and communicated a second change. In this song, he communicates that he wants his solo backed up by two-beat rhythm. This time, the pattern set up by the redundant communication —the message at all three levels and in several communication channels—is again reinforced throughout the rest of the performance. For example, Hodes's changes to 2/4 are theoretically uncomplex, and they were initiated at the beginning of new choruses. On the third song, when he started his solo, Hodes looked at the drummer and bassist, and when they looked back, he held up two fingers. Finally, when he started the 2/4, he "leaned on it", in effect overpowering anyone who might not have changed.

Evolutionary learning processes

Evolution, in biological theory, involves three stages or phases —variation, selection, and retention. An evolutionary view of the professional form seems to be appropriate, and therefore the selection devices must be identified. The musical aspect of group improvisation is not entirely free or random; on the level of the art form, chordal structure and the theory of chordal embellishment are among the selective devices that constrain the random variation (musical innovation) of individual behavior. On the level of the actual performance, two other types of selection devices can be seen: a) the conventions of breakpoints across all three tracks, and b) a strategy involving choice of repertoire and the introduction of variation.

In addition to musical conventions (level 1, macrostructure), social conventions such as communicative codes (level 2, integrative structure) serve as selective devices that constrain musical and social variation. Verbal remarks such as "fours" and "again" delimit the possible musical and social variation that follows. Similarly, nonverbal codes such as eye contact and hand gestures function as a selective device in group improvisation. Attention is the critical counterpart of code sending, for without proper attention on the part of the receivers, the coded message will not be received. The macrostructure and integrating structure levels both contain attention cues, points where innovation and change are most likely. It is important to note here that attention is on the others, not on one's own performance/response.

Moreover, it is interesting to note that the conservatism of the repertoire served an evolutionary purpose; it limited the amount of variation possible. While no musician was thinking in explicitly evolutionary terms, this simple device fits well into the event's evolutionary explanation. The songs became increasingly complex as the concert progressed, but they were simple early in the show. This again serves an interesting evolutionary purpose; it "stages" the generation of variation. As a way of conceptualizing this process, consider four players trying to find/establish a "center" that all were in, then varying from that center. Variations are tested and rejected or retained. If retained, they are solidified through repetition; then new variations are introduced. Although evolution is an appropriate and useful perspective on the group/organizational level, on an individual level, learning is how variations are retained. The central issue from the perspectives of the individual players is learning to accommodate to the idiosyncrasies and preferences of the others. Obviously, as new ideas are tried out by soloists, if they are to be retained, the individuals supporting the soloist must not only learn the preferences but also when they might be expressed.

Furthermore, the musical and social integrating structures that constrain task and social random variation are not independent, but they are embedded in one another. For example, music theories of chord structure and progression and phrase structure contain cues for timing attention and code sending. Musicians know, by virtue of musical theories and traditional conventions, when to send and expect to receive coded communication that in turn directs and constrains subsequent musical and social variation. Similarly, social conventions such as the verbal codes "fours," "goin' out," and "again" select operative musical conventions that in turn constrain subsequent musical and social variation.

In a turbulent environment (inherent in jazz) marked by personal uncertainty (inherent in zero-history groups), the function of selective devices can be seen as reducing uncertainty and constraining the turbulence of the environment. Group improvisation is thus neither entirely determined nor entirely random from both musical and social standpoints; improvisation is evolutionary in that it involves the selectively constrained retention of musical variation.

Implications

The implications of this case and analysis fall into three categories: first, implications of the practice of jazz for greater understanding of other human organizational contexts; second, the implications of using videotapes of jazz performances as the medium of data; and third, the implications of this study for jazz as a musical form.

Primarily, the field for many modern organizations, as in jazz, is basically turbulent and only marginally predictable (cf. Emery and Trist, 1979). In the concert, the field consisted of the musicians, the audience, and the rules and norms of the form. The individual musicians did not know what to expect from others or what they would have to do to maximize the outcome; they did not know what to expect from the audience; and they did not know what theoretical frames would or could be attempted. Individuals in other kinds of organizations face similar kinds of uncertainty as do jazz players during an improvised performance.

Structural constraints can be seen on two distinct levels: macrostructure (theory of practice) and the social/professional level. Recall that the macrostructure level in jazz consists in shared knowledge of musical theory, knowledge that serves as formally specified structural constraints on individual behavior in the process of producing music. Similarly, the macrostructure level in business consists of shared knowledge of constraints on the process of accomplishing business tasks, including such formally specified and coded structural constraints as legislation, industry regulation, governmental mandates, organizational mission statements, technical theories, and organizational plans, policies, and procedures. In both jazz and management, the social level of structural constraints on individual behavior involves relatively informal codes that concern interpersonal relations and communication. These shared social codes are akin to the notion of behavioral norms, a frequent topic of sociologists and anthropologists.

In this study we have seen the middle level—professional norms/social integrating structure—mediating between theory (macrostructure) and individual behavior. This integrative and normative level is, in this art form and industry, essential for the innovative and creative process. It is this level that informs the players of the probability of organizational action, especially changes in the structure of that action. It informs the individuals when a breakpoint might be approaching and what might be expected after it.

The second important observation coming from this analysis

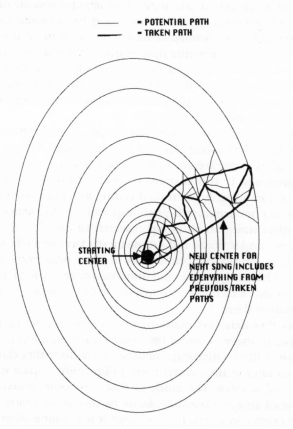

Figure 2.

has to do with the strategy used to draw the group together. Here, the repertoire served as a central part of the strategy, starting with a simple song, and becoming gradually more complex as the concert progressed. Along with this went decisions (informed by professional norms) of individual soloists to introduce novelty gradually and incrementally. These served both to keep all of the individuals operating most of the time in known territory by making the behavior of others relatively predictable. An example of this was Hodes's waiting until the third song to introduce his preference for 2/4 solos, but then maintaining that preference for the rest of the concert, using it every time he soloed.

This combination of communication, choice of task (moving from simple to complex), and personal predictability can be thought of as a "centering" strategy, in which the organization is drawn into a known center and coordinated there before moving into new territory. Such strategies have been seen to be useful in other organizations undergoing disjunctive change, as in learning to manage innovation or in mergers and acquisitions. Bastien (1987) points to such a strategy effectively implemented in a corporate acquisition. Kanter (1985) also discusses this kind of strategy in the management of change.

Among the most important issues coming from this study, however, is that the combination of this approach to jazz with videotaping gives us far greater insight into human social and task processes generally. In this case we were able to see a completed real social task in a highly controlled setting in its full complexity. This type of jazz performance is vastly superior to other social tasks in some critical ways. Much group research to date has involved simple, limited, and artificial tasks done by students in a laboratory. The limitations are obvious. Real tasks in most organizations are done by zero-history groups, and the tasks take so long that it would be boring, tedious, and costly to try to capture them on tape and analyze them.

Just as this data has caused us to resort to new methods and concepts to make sense of the event and to develop a much clearer sense of the relationships between all factors attending the event, so this kind of data could have a significant impact on the whole of social science. The study of this one event, showing all the richness of analysis available, leads us to call for many more similar jazz events, in a zero-history context with some other controls we had (other controls may also be available) and fully video-recorded. Nor can we diminish the importance of participant observers (musicians) being available to the researchers. Certainly essential to this study, it would be equally essential for others. The nature of the art form and the recording media are such that participant observers provide information not available without "inside" information, but this information explains the more observable and evaluable phenomena.

The history of jazz and jazz criticism is such that the focus has been on the soloist, with the notion that the solo is the creative aspect of a performance and that the background is relatively less important. What makes this study so interesting is that it has allowed the better observation of the nature of this relationship between foreground (the solo) and background (what the rest of the group is doing). We have seen that it is not appropriate to view jazz of this quality as a solitary solo performance against a stable, placid, and predictable background. What we propose as a necessary perspective is that we must understand creative and interesting jazz to come not from individual contributions but instead from the dynamic interplay between foreground and background.

Only on a simplistic and formal level is the soloist truly in charge of the artistic direction of the performance, for the solo is clearly both enabled and constrained by the background. It is inextricably enmeshed with the background. The background itself is both dynamic and complex *in the extreme!* In fact, the authors would argue that the critical difference between the solo and the background is largely a function of how the artists use the form to focus the attention of the audience, and not a function of the relative freedom or creative innovation of any single person. Creativity and innovation are a central and constant element of the work of all of the players at all times, not simply when they are soloing. Furthermore, the focus of the audience's attention is organized in the background, not in the foreground.

Parallels between jazz and management are strong here as in other aspects of jazz. A regular focus of research in management has focused on managers and managerial decisions in the way that jazz study and research has often focused on the solo and soloist. Clearly (at least to those of us who study management in the field) the social/organizational context of management in such that managers do not effectively make decisions outside of the overall context of the other "background" actors in their organizations (eg.: Bastien, 1987; Peters and Taterman, 1982). Thus, successful and creative action by managers is only possible within the creative context established by the less visible "sidemen" in businesses.

We end this essay with a dual call; first, that thinking about jazz return to understand the form first of all from the perspective of the entire group as a dynamic and creative entity, not just a soloist against a background. Secondly we would call for the study of management and organization from the same kind of perspective.

References

Bastien, David T. Common Patterns of behavior and communication in mergers and acquisitions. *Human Resource Management Journal.* 26 (1987): 17–34.

Bateson, Gregory. *Mind and Nature: A Necessary Unity.* New York: Bantam, 1972.

Bougon, M., Weick, K., & Binkhorst, D. Cognition in organizations: An analysis of the Utrecht Jazz Orchestra. *Administrative Science Quarterly.* 22 (1977): 606–09.

Emery, F. E., & Trist, E. L. *Towards a Social Ecology: Contextual Appreciations of the Future in the Present.* London: Plenum, 1975.

Kanter, Rosabeth M. *The Change Masters: Innovations for Productivity in the American Workplace.* New York: Simon and Shuster, 1985.

Peters, Thomas J. and Waterman, Robert H. *In Search of Excellence.* New York: Harper & Row, 1982.

Poole, M. Scott. Decision development in small groups, III: A multiple sequence model of group decision development. *Communication Monographs.* 50 (1983): 321–41.

Voyer, J. J. & Faulkner, R. R. Cognition and leadership in an artistic organization. *Proceedings of the 1986 Academy of Management,* 1986a, 160–64.

————. *Strategy and Organizational Cognition in a Simple Professional Bureaucracy.* Unpublished manuscript. Newark, NJ: Rutgers University, 1986b.

Weick, K. E., Gilfillan, D. P., & Keith, T. A. The effect of composer credibility on orchestra performance. *Sociometry.* 36 (1973): 435–62.

APPENDIX A
James Reese Europe, Discography

Organized under recording dates as follows:
1. Title.
2. Composer.
3. Matrix number, label and issue number.
4. Reissues:
    a. New World 260 "Shuffle Along" (NW260).
    b. New World 269 "Steppin' On The Gas" (NW269).
    c. Saydisc 221 (British) "Ragtime, Cakewalks & Stomps, Vol. 3: The Bands of Jim Europe and Arthur Pryor 'Too Much Mustard' (1907–1919)" (SDL221).
    d. Saydisc 253 "Ragtime, Cakewalks & Stomps, Vol. 4: 'Rusty Rags' (1900–1917)" (SDL253).
    e. RCA PM 42402 (French) "Ragtime Vol. 2: Cakewalks, Military Bands, Ragtime Orchestras, Coon Contests, Blues and Jazz (1900–1921)" (RCA42402).
5. U.S. Library Holdings (from *Rigler and Deutsch Index*): Syracuse University (NSY), New York Public Library (NN), Library of Congress (DLC), Yale University, (CTY), Stanford University (CST).

166

A. *Europe's Society Orchestra (1913–1914):*

Europe: Director
Cricket Smith: Cornet
Edgar Campbell: Clarinet
Tracy Cooper, George Smith, Walter Scott: Violins
Leonard Smith, Ford Dabney: Piano
Buddy Gilmore: Drums
5 Unk Banjos/Mandolins but may include: Opal Cooper,
    Lloyd Smith, William C. Elkins, Joe Meyers, George
    Waters, or Joe Grey

DECEMBER 29, 1913. NEW YORK

1. "Too Much Mustard/One-Step or Turkey Trot"
   Cecil Macklin
   (14246-1) Victor 35359-A, HMV 0230588 (as "Tres Moutarde")
   SDL221, RCA42402
   CTY, DLC, CST, NN
2. "Down Home Rag/One-Step or Turkey Trot"
   Wilbur C. Sweatman
   (14247-2) Victor 35359-B
   SDL221, RCA42402
   CTY, DLC, CST, NN
3. "Irresistible/Tango Argentine"
   L. Logatti
   (14249-1) Victor 35360-A
   None
   CTY, DLC, CST, NN
4. "Ampa/Maxixe Bresilien (Le Vrai)"
   J. Storoni
   (14248-1) Victor 35360-B
   None
   CTY, DLC, CST, NN

FEBRUARY 10, 1914. NEW YORK

Add: Chandler Ford: Cello
    George DeLeon: Baritone Horn
    Unk: Flute
Drop: All Banjo/Mandolins
1. "Congratulations Waltz (Castles' Lame Duck)"

167

James Reese Europe
(14435-1) Victor 35372-A
None
CTY

2. "Castle House Rag (Castles in Europe)"
James Reese Europe
(14433-3) Victor 35372-B
NW269, RCA42402
CTY, CST

Reese Europe-Ford T. Dabney
(14434-2) Victor 17553-A, HMV B-258
SDL253, NW269, RCA42402
CTY

4. "You're Here and I'm Here/One-Step"
Jerome D. Kern
(14432-1) Victor 17553-B
SDL253, RCA42402
CTY, NSY

OCTOBER 1, 1914. NEW YORK
Add: William Parquette: violin/vl ? Drop: 1 piano
1. "Fiora Waltz"
James Reese Europe
(15230-1-2) Victor rejected.
2. "Fox Trot"
(15231-1-2) Victor rejected.

B: *Lieut. Jim Europe's 369th Infantry ("Hell Fighters") Band*

Probably included:
Frank De Broite, Russell Smith, Pops Foster (not the bass
player), Jake Porter: Trumpets
Dope Andrews, Herb Flemming: Trombone
Pinkhead Parker: Alto Sax
Noble Sissle: Violin, Vocals
Battle Ax Kenny: Drums
And others

MARCH 3–7, 1919. NEW YORK
1. "Broadway Hit Medley"
a. Intro: "I've Got the Blue Ridge Blues"

    b. "Madelon" (Alfred Bryan & Camille Robert)

    c. "Till We Meet Again" (Richard Whiting)

    d. "Smiles" (J. Will Callahan & Lee S. Robert)

    (67470) PF (PatheFrere) 22082-A

    None

    NSY

2. "St. Louis Blues"
   W. C. Handy
   (67471) PF 22087
   None
   None

3. "How Ya Gonna Keep 'Em Down on the Farm?" vocal Walter Donaldson (words by Sam M. Lewis & Joe Young)
   (67472) PF 22080-A
   NW260
   DLC

4. "Arabian Nights"
   David/Hewitt
   (67473) PF 22080-B
   None
   CTY

5. "Darktown Strutters' Ball"
   Shelton Brooks
   (67475) PF 22081-A
   SDL221
   DLC

6. "Indianola"
   D. Onivas (ne Domenico Savino)
   (67474) PF 22081-B
   SDL221
   DLC

MARCH 7, 1919. NEW YORK

1. "That Moaning Trombone"
   Tom Bethel
   (67485) PF 22085-A, PA (Pathe Actuelle) 020929, PER (Perfect) 14111
   SDL221
   CST

2. "Memphis Blues"
   W. C. Handy

(67486) PF 22085-B, PA 020929, PER 14111
NW269, SDL221
CST

3. "Hesitating Blues"
W. C. Handy
(67481) PF 22086-B
SDL221
None

4. "Plantation Echoes" vocal
Coates
(67484) PF 22086-A
None
DLC

5. "Russian Rag"
(67487) PF 22087, PA 020928, PER 14110
Cobb
None

6. "Ja-Da"
Bob Carleton
(67488) PF 22082-B
None
NSY

MARCH 14, 1919. NEW YORK
Add: Creighton Thompson: vocal
1. "Jazz Baby" Thompson, vocal
Noble L. Sissle/James Reese Europe/Eubie Blake
(67517) PF 22103
None
CTY

2. "When the Bees Make Honey"
Walter Donaldson
(67520) PF 22103-B
None
CTY

3. "Mirandy" Sissle, vocal
Noble L. Sissle/James Reese Europe/Eubie Blake
(67515) PF 22089-A
NW260
CTY, DLC

4. "On Patrol in No Man's Land" Sissle, vocal

Noble L. Sissle/James Reese Europe
(67516) PF 22089-B
NW260
CTY, DLC

5. "All of No Man's Land is Ours" Sissle, vocal
    Noble L. Sissle/James Reese Europe
    (67518) PF 22104-A
    None
    CTY

6. "Jazzola" Sissle, vocal
    Robinson/Morse
    (67519) PF 22104-B
    None
    CTY

May 7, 1919. New York

1. "Dixie is Dixie Once More" Sissle, vocal
    Turner/Kard
    (67670) PF 22146-A
    None
    CTY, NSY

2. "That's Got 'Em"
    Wilbur C. Sweatman
    (67667) PF 22146-B
    None
    CTY, NSY

3. "The Dancing Deacon"
    UNK
    (67666) PF 22167
    None
    None

4. "Clarinet Marmelade"
    L. Shields/H. Ragas
    (67668) PF 22167, PA 020928, PER 14110
    NW269
    None

5. "Missouri Blues"
    Brown
    (67669) PF 22147-A
    None
    CTY, NSY

6. "My Choc'late Soldier Sammy Boy" Sissle, vocal
    Egbert Van Alstyne
    (67671) PF 22147-B
    None
    CTY, DLC

C. *Lieut. Jim Europe's Singing Serenaders:*

MARCH 18, 1919. NEW YORK

1. "Little David Play on Your Harp" Sissle, lead vocal
    Negro Spiritual
    (67478) PF 22084-A
    None
    CST, NSY
2. "Exhortation/Jubilee Song" Thompson, lead vocal
    Will Marion Cook
    (67477) Pathe 22084-B
    None
    CST, CTY, NSY
3. "Roll, Jordan, Roll"
    Negro Spiritual
    (67522) PF 22105-A, PA 020851-A, PER 11056
    None
    CST, DLC
4. "Ev'rybody Dat Talks About Heave' Aint' Goin' There"
    Unknown
    (?) PF 22105-B
    None
    DLC

D. *Jim Europe's Four Harmony Kings:*

Harold Browning, Horace Berry, Exodus Drayton, Roland
Hayes: Vocals

MAY 1919. NEW YORK

1. "Swing Low, Sweet Chariot"
    Negro Spiritual
    (67672) PF 22187, PA 020851-B, PER 11056

None
CST
2. "One More Ribber to Cross"
Negro Spiritual
(67673) PF 22187
None
None

APPENDIX B
Soviet Jazz, Discography

What follows is a list of the jazz records produced outside the Soviet Union by the musicians mentioned in the text. Leo Records are available through New Music Distribution Service, 500 Broadway, New York, NY 10012. East Wind Records are available from East Wind Trade Associates, 3325 17th St. NW, Washington, D.C. 20010. Records produced in the Soviet Union by Melodiya are sometimes available where Soviet materials are sold, such as Victor Kamkin Books in New York City and Rockville, Maryland.

Arkhangelsk, *Arkhangelsk* Leo 135
> Featuring Vladimir Rezitsky (saxophone)

Arsenel, *With Our Own Hands* East Wind 20649
> Led by saxophonist Alexei Kozlov.

Igor Brill, *Before the Sun Sets* East Wind 20646
> Pianist/composer Brill, with Alexander Oseichuk (saxophone)

Vladimir Chekasin, *Exercises* Leo 115
> With Sergey Kuryokin (piano) and Boris Grebenshchikov (guitar)

Vladimir Chekasin Quartet, *Nostalgia* Leo 119

Vladimir Chekasin Big Band, *New Vitality* Leo 142
The Ganelin Trio, *Catalogue, Live in East Germany* Leo 102
————, *Con Fuoco* Leo 106
————, *Ancora Da Capo, Part 1* Leo 108
————, *Ancora Da Capo, Part 2* Leo 109
————, *New Wine* Leo 112
————, *Vide* Leo 117
————, *Strictly for Our Friends* Leo 120
————, *Baltic Triangle* Leo 125
————, *Con Afetto* Leo 137
————, *Great Concerts in New Jazz: Taango . . in Nicklesdorf* Leo
      400/401
————, *Non Troppo* Hat Art 2027
————, *Poi Seque* East Wind 20647
      Vyacheslav Ganelin (keyboards), Vladimir Tarasov (percussion), and Vladimir Chekasin (saxes and clarinet)
Vyacheslav Ganelin, *Con Amore* Leo 147
Homer Liber, *Siberian 4* Leo 114
————, *Untitled* Leo 129
      Featuring Sergey Belichenko (drums, vibes) and Sergey
      Panasenko (bass, tuba)
Sergey Kuryokhin, *The Ways of Freedom* Leo 107
————, *Sentenced to Silence* Leo 110
      with Anatoly Vapirov (saxophone)
————, *Introduction to Popular Mechanics* Leo 146
————, *Pop Mechanics No. 17* Leo 158
      with Valentina Ponomareva, Igor Butman, Sergey Belichenko
      and Sergey Panasenko, the last two from Homer Liber
————, *Subway Culture* Leo 402/403
      with Boris Grebenshchikov
Alexei Kuznetsov, *Blue Coral* East Wind 20648
Vagif Mustafa-Zadeh, *Aspiration* East Wind 20650
      with Tamaz Kuraskvili (bass), Vladimir Boldyrev (drums), Elsa
      Mustafa-Zadeh (vocals)
Valentina Ponomareva, *Fortune Teller* Leo 136
————, *Intrusion* Leo 156
Anatoly Vapirov, *Invocations* Leo LR 121
      with Sergey Kuryokin and Valentina Ponomareva
————, *Macbeth* Leo 130
      with the Chamber Orchestra of the Leningrad Maly Theatre

Appendix B

Pyatras Vyshniauskas, *Inverso* Leo 140
with Vyacheslav Ganelin, Grigory Talas

In addition, there are two anthologies of interest:
A History of Jazz and Hot Dance in Russia (Harlequin 2012)
Includes original cuts of Alexander Tsfasman, Leonid Utsyosov, Eddie Rossner, and others. Harlequin Records are available from Daybreak Express Records, P.O. Box 250, Van Brunt Station, New York, NY 11215
Red Wave: Four Underground Bands from the U.S.S.R.
(Big Time 1-10020) A two-disc album of underground rock bands from Leningrad, one side each for Alisa, Kino, Strange Games, and Aquarium, with whom Sergei Kuryokin appears. Available from Stingray Productions, 9000 Sunset Blvd., Los Angeles, CA 90069.

APPENDIX C
Jazz and Modernism, Discography

For each time period presented in the essay, I have selected a few recordings representative of either particular artists mentioned or the broad styles described. Devotees of any one artist or style will no doubt argue with my choices, however, these should provide a good introduction and aural reference point for general readers and jazz aficianados alike.

In most cases an album has been listed, in others, specific cuts. Wherever possible, I have also noted when an artist's work appears on the Smithsonian Collection of Classic Jazz (SCCJ). This anthology is more likely to be available than are some of the original recordings themselves.

	1900 to 1920s: CLASSIC JAZZ
Louis Armstrong	Louis Armstrong and his hot five/Vol. 1 Columbia CL851 (some cuts on SCCJ, esp. "Struttin' with Some Barbeque" and "West End Blues"

Louis Armstrong and Earl Hines	Louis Armstrong and Earl Hines 1928 Smithsonian R 002 (esp. Armstrong-Hines duets)
Duke Ellington	The Indispensable Duke Ellington/Vols. 1, 2 French RCA/PM 43687 "Jazz Tribune" Series (esp. "Creole Love Call" and "Black and Tan Fantasy")
Duke Ellington	Works contained on the SCCJ (esp. two versions of "East St. Louis Toodleloo" [1927, 1937])

1940s: BEBOP

Dizzy Gillespie and Charlie Parker	Works contained on the SCCJ (esp. "Shaw Nuff," "Koko")
Dizzy Gillespie	The Development of an American Artist Smithsonian 2004
Charlie Parker	Bird: The Savoy Recordings Savoy 2201
Thelonious Monk	The Complete Blue Note Recordings Mosaic MR4-101 (some cuts on SCCJ)

1960s: "THIRD STREAM"

George Russell, Jimmy Giuffre, and Charles Mingus	Outstanding Jazz Compositions of the Twentieth-Century Columbia C2S 831 (also works by Harold Shapero, Milton Babbitt)
Gunther Schuller	Third Stream Music (with MJQ) Atlantic SD 1345 (esp. "Conversation")

1960s: "FREE JAZZ

Albert Ayler	Spiritual Unity esp. Disk 1002
Ornette Coleman	Free Jazz Atlantic S-1364 (excerpt on SCCJ)
John Coltrane	Ascension Impulse A-95

Archie Shepp	Fire Music
	Impulse A-86

1980s: "NEW DIRECTIONS"

Art Ensemble of Chicago	Nice Guys
	ECM 1-1126
Ornette Coleman	In All Languages
	Caravan of Dreams 85008 (features both the classic 1959 quartet in reunion and the current band, Prime Time)
Anthony Davis	Undine
	Gramavision 18-8612-1
George Russell	The African Game
	Blue Note BT 85103
Henry Threadgill	You Know the Number
	RCA/Novus 3013-1-N

INDEX

Abrams, Muhal Richard, 107
Abuladze, Tengiz, 67
Adorno, Theodor W., 130
Allen, Geri, 142
Anderson, Laurie, 105
Anderson, Pink, 86
Andrews, William, 45
Apollinaire, Guillaume, 95
Armstrong, Louis, 13, 38–59, 93–94, 98,
    103, 105, 113–17, 124–25, 133–35, 137
Art Ensemble of Chicago, 71–72, 74, 98,
    141
Astaire, Fred, 39
Attali, Jacques, 130
Ayler, Albert, 106, 139
Azarian, David, 76

Babayev, Rafik, 76
Baker, Houston A., 119
Balliett, Whitney, 48

Baquet, George, 118
Barban, Efim, 72, 76
Barker, Danny, 56, 113–17, 120–21, 124–25
Barnes, Clive, 90–91
Basie, Count, 86, 105
Bastien, Biddy, 150–56
Batashev, Alexey, 64, 68, 74
Baudue, Ray, 40
Bechet, Sidney, 50, 56, 62, 106, 113–19,
    121, 124–25
Beiderbecke, Bix, 42, 51, 90
Benford, Tommy, 87–89
Benjamin, Walter, 96–97, 100
Benton, Brook, 87
Berendt, Joachim, 67, 72
Bethell, Tom, 53
Bizet, Georges, 104
Blackwell, Scrapper, 86
Blake, Eubie, 23
Blake, Ran, 141

Index

Blakey, Art, 76
Bley, Carla, 142
Bolden, Buddy, 42, 120
Boldyrev, Vladimir, 76
Boulay, Steve, 72
Bowie, Lester, 106–7
Braxton, Anthony, 141
Brill, Igor, 66
Brown, Nappy, 87, 89
Brubeck, Dave, 68
Bruyninckx, Walter, 84
Brynn, J. Tim, 134
Bürger, Peter, 99–102, 105
Butman, Igor, 69
Byrne, David, 105

Cage, John, 97, 105, 107
Calinescu, Matei, 94, 103, 105, 129
Carnegie Hall, 22
Castle, Vernon and Irene, 23–24, 26–27, 32, 133
Cendrars, Blaise, 135
Chaloff, Serge, 105
Chekasin, Vladimir, 70
Cherry, Don, 76, 86, 141
Chopin, Frederic, 102
Clef Club Orchestra, 21–24, 134
Cocteau, Jean, 95
Cole, Bob, 21
Coleman, Ornette, 73, 76, 85, 93, 95, 98, 103, 106, 142
Collier, James Lincoln, 57, 84, 102
Collins, Lee, 56
Coltrane, Alice, 76
Coltrane, John, 75–76, 88, 139
Cook, Will Marion, 21
Corea, Chick, 76
Cotton Club, 42, 47
Crosby, Bing, 39

Dabney, Ford, 21
Davis, Anthony, 102, 141
Davis, Francis, 103
Davis, Miles, 74–75, 107
Davis, Reverend Gary, 86
Daye, Irene, 86
DeBroite, Frank, 27
DeFlores, Bob, 150

DeJohnette, Jack, 64
Delaunay, Charles, 84
Dennis, Stanley, 40
Dickerson, Carroll, 39
Dixon, Will, 20
Dodds, Warren "Baby," 56
Dolphy, Eric, 103
Dorsey, Tommy, 40
Duchamp, Marcel, 95, 100–101

East Wind Records, 76
Edel, Leon, 83
Ellington, Duke, 33, 63, 66, 97–98, 102, 106, 135
Ellison, Ralph, 57, 131
Europe, James Reese, 19–37, 133–34
Evans, Bill, 75

Fassbinder, Rainer Warner, 106
Feather, Leonard, 47, 83–84
Feigin, Leo (Leo Records), 69–70, 72–73
Foster, George "Pops," 56
Free, Ron, 89
Freeman, Bud, 40, 150–56

Gaillard, Slim, 85
Ganelin, Vyacheslav, 69, 73
Ganelin Trio, 61, 68–74, 141
Garanian, Georgii, 75
Gary, Sam, 87–88
Gauguin, Paul, 135
Gerlach, Horace, 40–43
Gershwin, George, 21, 93
Getz, Stan, 84
Giddens, Gary, 71, 94
Gillespie, Dizzy, 86, 89, 94, 104, 135, 137
Gilmore, Buddy, 20, 26
Ginsberg, Allen, 107
Gioia, Ted, 131
Gitler, Ira, 83
Glaser, Joe, 39, 54–55
Goodman, Benny, 22, 40, 63
Gorbachev, Mikhail, 67
Gordon, Dexter, 104
Gordon, Lorraine, 90
Gorky, Maxim, 62
Grainger, Percy, 92–94, 104
Grebenshchikov, Boris, 69

Green, Freddie, 89
Grieg, Edvard, 104
Gushee, Lawrence, 26, 121
Guys and Dolls, 90

Haden, Charlie, 74
Hamm, Charles, 31
Hammond, John, 39
Handy, W. C., 26, 28, 31, 121
Harper, Michael, 15
Harris, Craig, 107
Hawkins, Coleman, 105
Haydn, Franz Joseph, 101
Hellfighters, 29–32, 133
Henderson, Fletcher, 33, 39, 133
Hentoff, Nat, 13
Hindemith, Paul, 104
Hobsbawm, E. J., 14
Hodes, Art, 150–56, 159
Hoefer, George, 123
Hogan, Ernest, 20–21
Holder, Betty Jane, 52
Holland, Peanuts, 87
Honneger, Arthur, 104
Hopkins, Claude, 40
Horizon Press, 83
Howe, Jack, 87, 89–90
Hughes, Robert, 141
Hulei, Enrico, 20
Huyssen, Andreas, 106, 129

Ibraghimov, Takhir, 76
Ibrahim, Abdullah, 74
Institute of Jazz Studies (Rutgers University), 47
Ives, Charles, 102

Jackson, Ronald Shannon, 73
James, Harry, 63
Jarrett, Keith, 64
Jazzman, 64
Jenkins, Freddie, 102
Jenkins Orphanage (South Carolina), 87–90
Jepsen, Jorgen Grunnet, 84
Johnson, Bunk, 14, 117
Johnson, James Weldon, 20
Jones, Etta, 89

Jones, Jo, 13
Jones, King, 48
Joplin, Scott, 26
Jordan, Joe, 21

Karl, Frederick R., 130
Keepnews, Peter, 71
Kenney, William H., 15
Kern, Jerome, 25–26
Kernfeld, Barry, 92
Kersands, Billy, 44
Kirk, Rahsaan Roland, 76
Kitt, Eartha, 87
Kozlov, Alexei, 66
Kress, Karl, 40
Krupa, Gene, 86
Krushchev, Nikita, 64
Krutch, Joseph Wood, 129
Kurashvili, Tamaz, 76
Kuryokhin, Sergey, 69, 72
Kuznetsov, Alexei, 66

Ladies Home Journal, 134
Lang, Eddie, 42
Lateef, Yusef, 76
Leger, Ferdinand, 135
Leningrad Dixieland Jazz Band, 66, 68
Leppert, Richard, 130
Lewis, John, 97
Lewis, Mel, 64
Life magazine, 38, 54
Lincoln Gardens, 43, 49
Liszt, Franz, 102
Lloyd, Charles, 64
Lomax, Alan, 113, 122–23
Lundstrem, Oleg, 63
Lyotard, Jean-Francois, 106, 129

McClary, Susan, 130
McClure, Ron, 64
Macklin, Cecil, 24
McLaughlin, John, 76
McLean, Jackie, 88
Mahavishnu Orchestra, 66
Mahler, Gustav, 102
Mailer, Norman, 137
Manhattan Transfer, 76
Mardis Gras, 52

Index

Maytime Productions, 150
Medvedev, Alexander, 69, 74
Meierhold, Vsevolod, 62
Melodiya, 64, 68
Melody Maker, 53
Menville, Myra, 53
Meryman, Richard, 55, 57
Metheny, Pat, 66
Meyer, Leonard B., 130
Middleton, Velma, 56
Mikell, Eugene, 27
Miley, Bubber, 86
Milhaud, Darius, 135
Miller, Glenn, 87
Mingus, Charles, 15, 103, 105–6, 139–40
Modern Jazz Quartet, 102
Monk, Thelonius, 75, 94, 104, 135
Moody, James, 92, 94
Morduhaiev, Semen, 76
Morgan, Robert P., 130
Morgenstern, Dan, 47–48
Morris, Butch, 142
Morton, Jelly Roll, 33, 50, 103, 113–17, 121–26
Motley, Frank, 90
Murray, David, 106–7
Mustafa-Zadeh, Aziza, 76
Mustafa-Zadeh, Elza, 76
Mustafa-Zadeh, Vagif, 61, 66, 75–76

Namin, Stas, 68
Nanry, Charles, 131
Norvo, Red, 40

O'Day, Anita, 84, 86
O'Haire, Patricia, 71
Okeh Record Company, 39
Oliver, Joe "King," 41–43, 47, 49, 54, 103, 117, 133–34
Oliver, Stella, 51
Original Creole Band, 49
Original Dixieland Jazz Band, 42, 134
Orwell, George, 68
Ory, Kid, 133
O'Steen, Rex, 87–88
Ostendorf, Berndt, 130
Ott, Horace, 89–91

Pareles, Jon, 71
Parker, Charlie, 85, 92, 94, 103–5, 135
Parnakh, Valentin, 62, 64
Pasternak, Boris, 67
Pathe Record Company, 30–31
Pereversev, Leonid, 64
Perry, Ermitt, 87
Person, Houston, 89
Peterson, Oscar, 75
Petit, Buddy, 53
Peyton, Benny, 62
Picabia, Francis, 135
Picasso, Pablo, 95, 135
Picou, Alphonse, 104–5
Pollock, Jackson, 107
Ponomoreva, Valentina, 69
Popular Mechanics (Soviet Orchestra), 70
Princeton Triangle Club Jazz Band, 90
Prysock, Arthur, 89
Purim, Flora, 76
Pushen, Grigori, 76

Radano, Ronald, 98
Randolph, Zilner, 41
Red Flag Baltic Fleet Jazz Orchestra, 63
Richardson, "Jazz Lips," 43
Robeson, Paul, 105
Rockwell, John, 130
Rogers, Timmy, 84
Rose, Al, 121
Rosner, Eddie, 63–64
Rossini, Gioacchino, 102, 104
ROVA Saxophone Quartet, 68, 72
Russell, Al (Stomp), 84, 87
Russell, George, 142
Russell, Luis, 39
Russell, Sammy, 122
Rust, Brian, 84

Satie, Erik, 95
Saulsky, Yuri, 66, 74
Schaefer, John, 130
Schnabel, Artur, 97
Schorske, Carl, 129
Schuller, Gunther, 25, 31, 130
Shattuck, Roger, 130
Shead, Richard, 130

Shepp, Archie, 140
Sims, Zoot, 64
Sissle, Noble, 23, 27–28, 31
Six Brown Brothers, 25
Small, Drink, 89–90
Small's Paradise, 42
Smith, Cricket, 26
Smith, Hal, 150
Smith, Jabbo, 86–90
Smith, Willie "the Lion," 114–17, 120, 123–25
Squirrel Ashcraft's House of Jazz, 90
Stalin, Josef, 60, 62
Starr, S. Frederick, 61–63, 72, 74
Stepto, Robert, 40
Stone, Albert, 40
Stravinsky, Igor, 95, 104
Sun Ra, 70, 72, 84, 141
Sweatman, Wilber, 24

Tarasov, Vladimir, 70
Tate, Erskine, 39
Taylor, Billy, 68
Taylor, Cecil, 93, 95, 98, 106
Thompson, Creighton, 31
Threadgill, Henry, 107, 141
Tillich, Paul, 139
Tom Sawyer (Mark Twain), 45
Tsfasman, Alexander, 62–64
Tyers, William, 21
Tzara, Tristan, 95

Ullman, Michael, 88
Ulmer, James "Blood," 73, 86, 88
University of South Carolina Jazz and Blues Archives, 86
Utyosov, Leonid, 62–64

Vallee, Rudy, 40, 42
Vapirov, Anatoly, 69
Varese, Edgar, 104
Venuti, Joe, 40
Vernon, Grenville, 30
Victor Talking Machine Company, 24, 42
Vodery, Will, 21
Voice of America, 63

Walker, George, 21
Weather Report, 66
White, Josh, 86
Whiteman, Paul, 22, 40
Willett, John, 129
Williams, Bert, 21
Williams, Johnny, 86, 89
Williams, Martin, 142
Williams, William Carlos, 14

Young, Lester, 93, 105
Young, Webster, 88–89